Communication Skills for Rural Development

Evans Books for Rural Development

TROPICAL FIELD CROPS
FRUIT AND VEGETABLES
COMMUNICATION SKILLS FOR RURAL DEVELOPMENT

Evans Books for Rural Development

COMMUNICATION SKILLS FOR RURAL DEVELOPMENT

Ian MacDonald
and
David Hearle

Evans Brothers Limited

Published by Evans Brothers Limited
2A Portman Mansions, Chiltern Street
London W1M 1LE

Evans Brothers (Nigeria Publishers) Limited
PMB 5164, Jericho Road
Ibadan

Evans Brothers (Kenya) Limited
PO Box 44536
Nairobi

© Ian MacDonald and David Hearle 1984
Illustrations © Evans Brothers Limited 1984
All Rights Reserved. No part of this publication may
be reproduced, stored in a retrieval system, or transmitted
in any form or by any means, electronic, mechanical,
photocopying, recording or otherwise, without the prior
permission of Evans Brothers Limited.

First published 1984

Illustrated by Patrice Aitken

Printed by BAS Printers Limited,
Over Wallop, Stockbridge, Hampshire
ISBN 0 237 50791 9

Contents

Introduction — vii

1 **The Change Agent in the rural community** — 1
Community participation in planning development activities; Extension, origin and definitions; The role of the Change Agent; Problems which the Change Agent faces

2 **Messages and innovations** — 16
Communication principles; Audience perception; Non-verbal communication; The adoption process; Barriers to communication; Target audiences; The innovation or message; Selecting messages

3 **Communication methods** — 34
Different communication methods; Individual visits; Mass media; Traditional channels; Village meetings; Study visits for farmers; Demonstrations; Group work

4 **Using audio-visual aids** — 47
Communications media; Advantages and disadvantages of media; Teaching with audio-visual aids; Visual aid design; Production of written materials; Pre-testing audio-visual materials; Operation, care and maintenance of equipment

5 **Teaching methods and skills** — 69
Classroom teaching; Teaching adults; Planning; Presentation

6 **Managing training courses** — 80
Is a course really necessary; Pre-course planning; Introductory session; Audio-visual materials for courses; Training records and evaluation

7 **Supervising staff** — 90
A manager's job; Management styles; Activities of supervisors

8 **Planning and evaluating programmes** — 100
National aims; Needs assessment; Resources of the area; Analysis of data; Programme objectives; Technical information; Work planning; Evaluation

9 **Rural development strategies** — 112
Inputs and services to assist development; Provision of services; Constraints to development; Development strategies; Assumptions about Extension

Introduction

There are thousands of men and women all over the world who are working to improve the standard of living of rural families. These people are bringing about improvements in health, nutrition, farming, forestry, fishing or in related subjects. They are given a variety of names, such as family planning workers, community development officers, health advisers, extension workers and so on. In this book the term 'Change Agent' is used to cover all these titles.

We consider the subject matter of the book will be useful for all those working in rural development, be they in natural resources, health, community development, the T & V system of extension or general extension.

Most Change Agents have had a period at high school and have undertaken two or three years of technical training. However, to be effective in their work, Change Agents must combine this technical knowledge with communications skills. Generally, the training they receive is almost entirely concerned with providing technical knowledge. The result is that an Agent may be capable of solving some of the problems which rural people are experiencing, yet not be able to communicate or convince them of this.

During the last few years in many countries, there has been a rapid increase in recruitment of Change Agents, resulting in organizations which now have considerable manpower, but are sometimes unable to achieve really significant development results. What is often lacking in these new recruits is a real commitment to helping the rural poor, and without this attitude any development plans will fail.

This book is concerned with both the attitudes and communication skills required by Change Agents and we believe that a careful study of its contents will be of benefit to these people, particularly at the beginning of their careers.

Each chapter of the book is presented in a way which will help the reader to study the material. The chapter starts with the learning objectives and definitions of technical terms that are used. This is followed by an introduction which provides reasons why the subject is important and briefly discusses its theoretical foundation. Then, after the subject matter itself, there are study questions and group exercises which are designed to help the reader think further about the subject.

We are grateful to Andrew Bartlett who not only made many comments and suggestions, but who also undertook the editing of this book.

Ian MacDonald
David Hearle

1 The Change Agent in the rural community

Rural communities may well be capable of defining their own problems. They may not always be aware of what improvements can be made within the community, nor be able to define solutions to their problems. Thus Change Agents should function as helpers and advisers: they should not be there to give instructions about the development of the communities.

It is important to make clear what the terms 'rural development' and 'Extension' mean, what is the role of the Change Agent and what are the problems that he or she faces.

Objectives

At the end of this chapter you should be able to:
  (a) Discuss the necessity of participation by a local community in planning.
  (b) Describe the role of the Change Agent.
  (c) List the personal qualities which could assist him in his work.
  (d) Discuss the main problems he may face.

Definitions of words used

attitude — thought, feeling, belief of person about something
empathy — ability to think and feel as another person does; process of projecting oneself in imagination into the personality of another
principle — a reason by which action may be guided
participation — a shared common action
role — a task or function of a person

Introduction: Community participation in planning development activities

Ideally, people should identify their own needs and problems. However, in a development situation where they come into contact with ideas and techniques beyond the scope of their traditional knowledge, outside assistance is often necessary. Assistance means giving help, not controlling, and so when planning is being undertaken it should be with the full participation of the community.

It is sometimes assumed that rural people are not very clever and have to be told what to do all the time. The facts are really rather different. Rural people have survived for centuries, generally living in harmony with the environment and successfully conducting their own affairs, wanting little other than to be left in peace. This is not to say there were not times of hardship caused by feudal landlords, droughts or pests.

However, in the early part of this century the pressure of increasing population and the desire for increased material goods began to upset the balance, both socially and with regard to the natural resources.

During the last 30 years, governments and international agencies have been concerned about this imbalance and about the need to feed cheaply the ever-expanding town populations. Thus they started to implement massive development schemes. Some of these schemes have not succeeded, and it is important for us to realize why they have not succeeded so that we do not continue to make the same mistakes.

Past experience of rural people with outsiders has usually been unsatisfactory. Officials and traders have often been concerned with taxation or exploitation, and the money raised has seldom been used to benefit the rural areas. This has left a legacy of mistrust, and this is the legacy with which we, as Change Agents, now have to contend.

Recently government authorities have decided in general what should be done to improve the position of rural people. But the plans may not always be accepted by the rural people as being what they want or need. Failure to consult the local population causes great resentment, hostility and suspicion. Indeed, going to a farmer or community with a ready-made plan for them to follow, without prior consultation, displays a lack of understanding of human nature. To assume, because of our education and training, that we know better is arrogant. Education does not necessarily create wisdom. We may know certain new technical matters, but we do not know the local constraints and may be ignorant of local farming conditions.

Also, from a psychological point of view, people need to be involved in the planning of their own lives and activities. If they are not involved in this way, they cannot be expected to co-operate.

Such points apply to large communities, to villages, or to individual farmers, and should give us guidance in determining the principles which we should follow.

'Extension' origin and definitions

This book is concerned with methods and techniques used in rural development, and this term must be explained. The word most often used to describe rural development fieldwork is 'Extension'.

Scotland was one of the first countries to start an 'extension' service when the universities decided to 'extend' their educational efforts beyond the university boundaries, although the term 'extension education' was introduced in Cambridge University. The concept was then taken up in the USA, particularly in the agricultural field. There, graduates were employed to work in the rural areas under the guidance of a nearby university. Their job was to introduce new ideas and skills to farmers. Since then, 'Extension' has spread to almost all countries in the world.

It was fairly quickly realized that simply telling people about a discovery or innovation was not sufficient. For people to accept an innovation (a new idea), not only does their knowledge have to change, but also their attitudes, especially if they live in a traditional, conservative community. Many of these people are suspicious of government workers and strangers, so trust and friendship need to be built up. It is often necessary to work through the village elders or leaders. If this is not done, there may be social problems caused by the threat to the village leadership and its social structure, in which case the community is likely to reject any help offered.

As the need for services other than those in the field of agriculture was realized, Extension organisations were also developed in health, family planning, fisheries, forestry, etc. The term 'Extension' has not been so frequently used to describe these organizations although they serve the same essential functions, as can be seen from the following definitions:

'People must first change their attitude to change before they can accept new ideas.'

'To bring about a change in attitude is a basic educational function of extension.' (*ibid.*)

'An extension worker seeks out and encourages people to change their traditional attitudes towards development and helps them achieve a better standard of living.' (*ibid.*)

'All forms of extension take education to the people.' (*ibid.*)

'... to teach people to raise their standard of living, by their own efforts, using their own resources of manpower and materials, with the minimum of assistance from governments. By encouraging local leadership and a spirit of self help ...' A. Savile

'... to help people solve their own problems through the application of scientific knowledge.'

'A service or system which assists farm people, through educational procedures, in improving farming methods and techniques, increasing production efficiency and income, bettering their levels of living, and lifting the social and educational standards of rural life.' A. H. Maunder, FAO

Ronald Havelock in *Training for Change Agents* suggests that there are four primary ways in which a person can act as a Change Agent. He suggests that the Change Agent should provide:

(a) Motivation – stimulus and pressure to make rural people aware of development benefits.

(b) Technical advice – technical solutions at the time they are required.
(c) Problem solving – help in problem identification and solving.
(d) Resources – knowledge about assistance from agencies and governments, where inputs, credit and expertise can be obtained.

Extension work, then, is seen by different people as being different things, though all are related. Some see it as attitude changing, some as a more educational operation, and others as a service or system for supplying the technology which rural development requires.

The next question therefore is, what is the role of the Change Agent?

The role of the Change Agent

The Change Agent is mainly working on his own and, as he is often a comparative stranger, he is liable to be criticised by the local community for any shortcomings.

Therefore, he must be aware of how he should proceed in order to be accepted and effective. The main considerations are:

(a) To get to know the community and the leaders, and to be friendly.
(b) To know the area, its problems, and the needs of the community.
(c) To study the technical knowledge needed by the rural people so that any information given is accurate.
(d) To be aware of the likely costs and profitability of any innovations.
(e) To encourage people to take up those innovations most likely to work, which cost little and give a fair return. Long term, expensive and risky new ideas should not be suggested.
(f) To accept that the rural people know a great deal about the problems in their area, and that they will suggest sensible ideas about improvement, provided they are encouraged to do so.
(g) Know about government, private organizations and local development plans, and where help can be obtained.

In addition he or she should have a liking for rural people, be interested in local affairs, and should want to work with people and share knowledge and ideas.

He will also need to be a good communicator, public speaker (see Figure 2), a good teacher, and be skilful in encouraging local leaders to take an active part in development.

Problems which the Change Agent faces

The Agent is usually hampered in his work by certain constraints and problems. He will be better able to overcome them if he is aware of what these are. In particular, his position is difficult, as he is expected

Figure 1 Social considerations in extension planning

Traditional attitudes of rural families

Possible help from religious leaders

Local opinion about government officials

Standard of education

Desire for change

Strength of village power elite

Figure 2 The poor public speaker

to carry out various orders from his superiors while also taking account of the requirements of the rural community. Other problems are:

(a) **Problems related to the local community**

1. *Rivalry within the village between families*
The Change Agent will have to be equally friendly with all the families and show no bias.

2. *The difficulty of working with very poor farmers with whom one has little empathy*
Poor farmers also have difficulty in relating to Change Agents. However, regular visits will create better understanding and friendships.

Figure 3   Empathy

Change Agent

has empathy towards:	*may have little empathy towards:*
Progressive farm families	Poor farmers
Landlords	Landless people
School teachers	Small tenant farmers
Government officials	Poor fishermen
Large fishing boat owners	
Village leaders	

---

3. *The traditional attitudes of some rural communities towards development*
An attitude is a tendency to think in a particular way about something. Attitudes are built up over many years and reinforced by experience. Thus it is very difficult for someone to change his ideas if his circumstances and environment remain the same.

If, for example, a farmer has always grown a particular crop, like maize, and got a good price for it, he is unlikely to be persuaded to grow something else. If, however, the price of maize falls, if his friends laugh at him for growing it, or something else pays better, then his environment has changed and he is likely to change his attitude to maize growing. Thus persuasion alone may have little effect. What is needed is an environmental change.

(b) **Problems related to the development organization**

4. *Miscellaneous duties*
These might include undertaking a crop census, compiling reports, etc. These administrative and regulatory duties may have to be done as part of the Agent's job but he should try and keep the time spent on them to a minimum.

5. *The Change Agent receiving what he considers a low rate of pay and needing to earn additional money*
There is little he can do about his pay; however, he can run a good

Figure 4   Attitudes change because conditions change

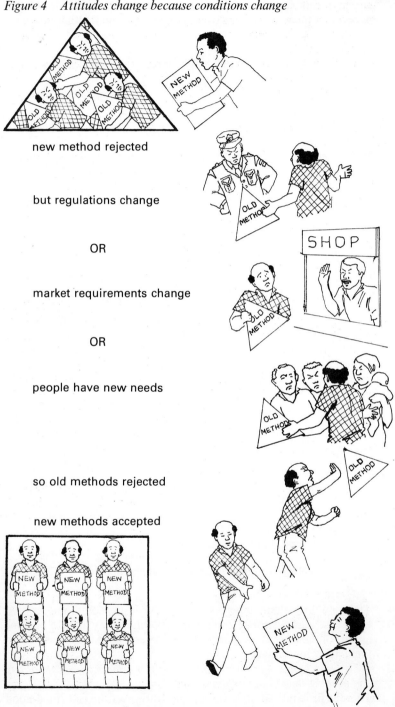

new method rejected

but regulations change

OR

market requirements change

OR

people have new needs

so old methods rejected

new methods accepted

garden and thereby feed himself and his family well. In this way he may in fact be better off than many government workers in town.

6. *The idea, in some societies, that government officials are very important people*

This can lead to farm families impoverishing themselves to provide lavish meals or presents for the Agent. It can also lead to bribery and exploitation. All these things will destroy any Extension efforts.

Self-study questions

1. Why should a Change Agent be an adviser rather than an instructor?
2. What attitudes does the Change Agent need?
3. What initial steps should a new Change Agent take in his area?

Group activity studies

Empathy Game

Objective

This activity is undertaken in order to obtain a better understanding of the difference between Change Agents and rural families, and to consider how these can be overcome.

Method

In the table below is a list of characteristics which describe most Change Agents. Fill in the other columns with those characteristics which you think describe rural families by comparison with the Change Agent. For example, progressive families are those prepared to accept new ideas and so might well be educated, whereas average families would probably not be educated.

Change Agent	Progressive Families	Average Families
Educated		
Trained		
Interested in town activities		
Wide interest in national events		
Interested in sport		

Figure 5   Some difficulties for Change Agent

Jealousies between village families

Too much office work and not enough time in field

Should decline gifts from poor families and grow his own vegetables

Has regular sums of money to spend		
Modern in outlook		
Friendly towards strangers		

Conclusion
Discuss the differences and how the gaps can be overcome.

Bottle Game

Change Agents have many problems, and it is important to establish who is responsible for solving them. To look at these problems and at your responsibility as a Change Agent, you can play the 'Bottle Game'.

The game has been used very successfully in a number of different situations in Kenya, Nepal, Thailand and Bangladesh. It can be played with colleagues, and used at the start of a training course for Change Agents. Some three hours should be allowed for the game and not more than 15 people should take part.

Objectives
The game achieves the following:
 (a) It identifies the different people involved in a specific development situation.
 (d) It identifies the obstacles and problems faced by each of these people.
 (c) It lists their activities.
 (d) It identifies those problems which are the responsibility of the participants.

Materials required
 (a) About 60 wooden blocks (suggested size 8 × 8 × 12 cm).
 (b) Objects which will represent the various groups of people involved, i.e., farmers, public, schools, Change Agents, district/divisional officers, ministry headquarters, research station, mass media producers. The objects could be bottles, cardboard tubes, etc., each one having a label on it stating which group it represents.
 (c) Blackboards, large sheets of paper, marker pens, large table.

Method
 Step 1: Participants decide on the relevant groups of people in their development situation, e.g., local leaders, research organizations, Change Agents, farmers, etc. There will probably be some 6–10 groups chosen.

Figure 6   The Bottle Game

Step 2: Label the bottles or objects with the names of the groups which were decided in Step 1.

Step 3: Participants then decide on the layout of the bottles on the table. For instance, how close are farmers to research or ministry to Change Agents?

Step 4: Have a large sheet of paper or a blackboard available for each group to be considered. Participants then discuss the problems each group has. These problems are written down as lists for each group. Participants have to display considerable empathy for each group to determine what the problems are.

The wooden blocks, each one of which represents a problem, are built up like a wall around each bottle. The Change Agent bottle will probably be totally surrounded by its wall.

Step 5: Take each group's list in turn and decide who is responsible for solving each problem. Mark this on the lists.

Generally problems move upwards. This is to say that the problems of the Change Agents are most often the responsibility of the more senior officers, while some of the farmers' problems become the Change Agent's responsibility. Sometimes there may be a joint responsibility between two groups. For instance, the problem of lack of technical information possessed by farmers may be the responsibility of Change Agents and the information unit, and possibly the farmers themselves.

Do not spend time on deciding how actually to solve these problems. Solutions will be sought later.

Guide for Bottle Game (for organizers only)

The following table is a list of possible problems and who might be responsible for them. This is only a guide for the organizer and should not be shown to the participants. Only those responsible for the Change Agents' problems have been filled in here, as an example. The participants should discuss and fill in the 'responsibility' column for all the problems.

Change Agents

Problems	*Responsibility*
Little transport	Ministry
Little empathy with poor farmers	Training officer/Change Agents themselves
Work in isolation	District officer
Poor management/ organization	District officer
Lack of technical information	Information unit/Change Agents
Poor communication with superior officer/ministry	District officer
Difficult to contact women, who do much of the farming	Change Agent
Personal and family needs conflicting with work	?

Own farm activities or business conflicting with work	?
Dishonesty of some staff creating lack of confidence	District officer
No funds for photos, posters, etc.	Ministry
Poor housing	Ministry
Poor morale	Everyone
Some staff drink too much	District officer
No in-service training	Training officer
No media for farmers	Information officer
Transfer too frequent	Ministry
Language and culture problems	Ministry postings and Change Agents

School teachers and pupils

Problems	*Responsibility*
Lack of agricultural information	?
Lack of visits by Change Agents	
Lack of labour in schools (e.g., to look after projects during school vacations)	

Research workers

Problems	*Responsibility*
Insufficient information regarding farmers' problems	?
Little attempt to contact farmers	
Lack of channels for dissemination	
Findings not in a digestible form	

Poorer rural people

Problems	*Responsibility*
Only women and old men available for work	?
Given wrong information or very little information	
Do not meet Change Agents	
Cannot read	
Have no radios	
Do not go to meetings	
No visits by film units	
No money	

Discussion
Finally a discussion should be held on what participants have learnt. During the game the participants may discover:
(a) They normally spend a great deal of time working on activities that have little relationship to the goals of their organization.
(b) They spend considerable time on problems which are not solvable by them.
(c) They need to communicate more effectively with those who can solve these problems.
(d) Most important, which problems are their specific responsibilities.

2 Messages and innovations

This chapter is concerned with how messages are accepted, and the barriers to good communication.

Objectives

At the end of this chapter you should be able to:
(a) Explain what communication is.
(b) State in what way a message should be suitable for an audience.
(c) Describe the adoption process.
(d) List some of the barriers to good communication.
(e) Explain 'feedback'.
(f) List some non-verbal communication actions.

Definitions of words used

adopt	take up, accept
channel	means of passing or conveying
communicate	to impart, to transmit, to share
comprehension	taking in understanding
evaluate	find or state value of, measure
feedback	response to a message, knowledge of the results of the communication
innovation	new idea or technique
message	specific piece of information, communication of an idea, instruction or request
non-verbal communication	communication between people through expressions and actions, without using words
perceive	observe, understand
perception –	understanding, comprehension
receiver	one who accepts (the message)
sender	one who gives out (the message)
technically correct	scientifically proven
Subject Matter Specialist (SMS)	worker with special expertise, who supports the Change Agent

Introduction: Communication principles

Change Agents spend a considerable amount of their time giving out and sometimes sending out information to rural people. However, this often becomes a one-way communication flow, and the messages are liable to turn into commands and not true communications.

A communication can be defined as 'a means of exchanging messages or an act of giving information and receiving a response'. For a message to be part of a communication there has to be a sender and also a person who receives the message – who actually hears it and responds to it. If it is just a noise which is ignored, then it has not been received.

We can now consider on what communication principles we should base our work. These could include:

(a) Rural people need to be informed about new ideas.

(b) Communication should start with rural people expressing their needs and wishes.

(c) The messages must be suited to these needs of the rural people, and not to government information needs. (There are other organizations for this.)

(d) Many channels of communication should be used to impart ideas and information.

(e) The rural community is made up of many different groups of people, and these groups (target audiences) have different information and motivation requirements.

Audience perception

When we communicate we have to consider how much the audience will understand or perceive.

Firstly, if the ideas are too difficult then there will be little comprehension.

Secondly, if the words are too complex, the audience will not understand. Sometimes our audience will have a different meaning for a particular word than our own. Different words create different images in people's minds. Consider, for example, such words as 'quickly', 'education', 'house', 'frequently'.

Thirdly, to make things even more complicated, a person will only perceive what he subconsciously wants to perceive. In all of us there are mental 'screens', whereby we not only reject, but also we do not even see or hear information which we do not want to perceive. This is called 'selective perception'. Selective perception can be based on interest or cultural or emotional factors. Therefore we need to know what our audience is interested in, so that we can make our communications more acceptable.

Figure 7 Communications

Incomplete communication

Sender ⟶ Message ⟶ Receiver

Complete communication

Analysis of a communication
Who says what to whom and with what response?

Non-verbal communication

A very important part of our communications with other people is non-verbal: it does not involve words. Non-verbal communication helps in establishing good inter-personal relationships. These relationships depend to a large extent on the degree of warmth expressed by those communicating with each other. If a speaker is unfriendly, he is unlikely to create a good relationship. The person who is warm and friendly, however, will easily gain trust and friendship. This can be done not only by the tone of voice and the use of polite and well chosen words, but also by body movement or body language. Through your 'body language' response you can actually influence what a person is saying to you or even cause him to cease speaking altogether. For example, if you turn your body away from him and stop looking at him, he will lose confidence and become very uncertain. Here are some of the common non-verbal signs we make when communicating:

Figure 8   Non-verbal communication

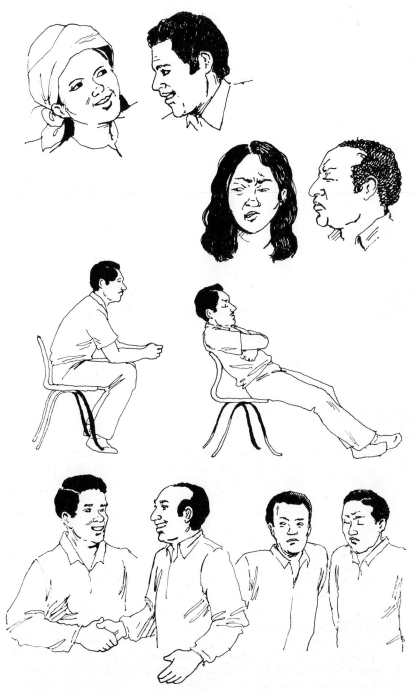

Encouraging body language	Discouraging body language
Smile	Frown
Wink (friendliness)	Eyebrows lifted in disbelief
Wide-open eyes, eyes widening at something pleasant	Half-closed eyes (lack of interest)
Eye contact (showing interest)	Look away all the time (not interested)
Relaxed mouth	Compressed lips, teeth clenched,
Relaxed movements	Stiff, showing boredom
Attentive expression	Tap fingers (impatience)
Lean towards person	Lean back, away from the person
Turn towards person	Turn body away from person
Warm handshake	Cold, weak greeting
Arm around shoulder, pat on back	No touching, no physical contact at all
Little noises of encouragement like 'uh-huh' or 'um'	Total silence, giving no encouragement
	Clasped arms to isolate or protect oneself
	Shaky hands, trembling legs (fear)

Note: These signs may vary somewhat from culture to culture.

Other body language considerations:

(a) Our facial expressions can show many feelings such as hate, sadness, boredom, fear, amusement, happiness.

(b) Everyone feels they want some space around them in normal social contact. This is usually several feet at least. If people come closer we feel uncomfortable and embarrassed. We consider this area around us as our territory, in the same way that animals have territories around them which they defend.

(c) It is normally polite to look people in the eye when talking to them, but not for too long, unless you are sitting some distance away.

(d) When you are in your office and you have a visitor it is considered to be fairly formal to remain behind your desk. If it is not just a business visit you should get up and go round the desk to meet him.

(e) Body signals are not always what they appear to be. This also depends on the situation. Some body movements are done quite deliberately by the person, other movements may be done unconsciously.

The adoption process

Any person, when he hears of a new idea, will go through a number of stages before he adopts the idea. This is called the 'adoption process'. The Change Agent needs to be aware of these stages and he should not try to hurry the person through them. The stages are:

(a) Awareness – A person first learns about a new idea, product or practice. He has only general knowledge about it and knows nothing of its special qualities or its usefulness.

(b) Interest – At this stage the person is not satisfied with just knowing that the idea exists. He wants more detailed information about what it is, what it will do and how it will work. He will listen and read about it and seek more information.

(c) Evaluation – He evaluates all the information he has and decides whether the new idea is good for him.

(d) Trial – Once he decides he likes the idea, he will give it a trial. This may be for a long period of time or on a limited scale.

(e) Adoption – This is the stage where he firmly adopts the idea and then may even encourage others to do so.

Figure 9: The adoption process

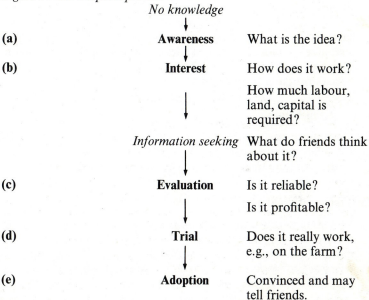

The idea can be rejected at any stage.

Barriers to communication

There are a number of constraints which may prevent people adopting a new idea. Some are discussed below.

Lack of awareness

A person may not listen to the idea because basic needs are not being satisfied. For example, he is hungry, cold, thirsty or hot. He may be worried about other matters – family, health, money.

No interest

The idea may not be compatible with other interests or attitudes. He may not want to do a particular activity even if profitable, e.g., he rejects a suggested innovation like keeping milk cows, if he does not like livestock work. Some innovations may also be socially unacceptable in some countries, or amongst a certain class or caste of people, e.g., cutting sugar cane or handling manure.

Cannot adopt

Here he may not have the capital or labour to adopt the idea. Other constraints may prevent him, such as lack of water, high rates of interest, etc. The Green Revolution demonstrated clearly that rich farmers can adopt new ideas much more quickly than the poorer farmers; obviously information is not all that is needed to bring about adoption.

It used to be thought that it was the mental characteristics of the farmer which made him begin to adopt. However, it is probably true that most farming people will adopt new ideas if they are convinced that they will benefit from them and if they are not hampered by social or organizational constraints.

Incorrect messages

Communication means that something is believed and undertaken. If the information is incorrect, then there is a danger that nothing in future from the same source will be believed. It will be ignored.

Too much information

Providing effective information is a matter of economy. The fewer facts presented, provided they are complete, the better the information. An overload of information leads to confusion. It is necessary to work out how much information is needed.

Insufficient feedback

Feedback is the response that an audience or person gives to the speaker. This feedback enables the sender to modify his message. In a talk between two people the responses, both verbal and non-verbal, enable each person constantly to monitor and modify what they say.

Where the feedback is not received until after the message has been completed, then the feedback has to be used to modify the next production. This could be the situation, for example, at a public meeting or a film show.

If there is no feedback, then misunderstandings between the sender and the receiver may develop until there is no effective communication at all.

Barriers to communication (Figure 10)

Non-reception
Low volume of sound.
Poor sound quality, poor visual quality.
Lack of equipment, radio, TV, film, print material.
Little dissemination of information between people.
Person cannot read, does not listen to others reading.

Comprehension failure
Different language.
Unsuitable words.
Difficult ideas.

Preoccupation
Hungry, thirsty.
Uncomfortable.
Cold or hot.
Tired or overworked.
Personal worries.
Concern about other tasks.

Selective perception
Message rejected because of:
little interest in the message,
unusual form or style,
cultural aspects,
religious aspects.

Communicator failure
Unusual appearance of communicator.
Superior attitude of communicator.
Badly produced message.
Badly presented message.
Unsuitable message.
Too much communication.

Target audiences

We may at some time want to send a message to all the rural community. At other times we may wish to contact a specific group. Such a group is called a 'target audience'.

Obviously we should not assume that all the rural people are interested in every message or that they might all equally understand a message. Every community can be divided up into groups. A possible breakdown might be: landless labourers; poor, medium and rich farmers; landlords; school teachers; businessmen; local leaders; religious leaders; school children; poor women; medium income and rich women; and so on. The division for some purposes might be on educational lines, such as illiterate, primary, secondary, etc., or according to activities, e.g., cattle owners, cotton growers, vegetable producers.

Before we can start sending messages to our selected target audience we need to know considerably more about the audience. Figure 11 shows the main characteristics we might need to know.

Figure 10   Barriers to communication

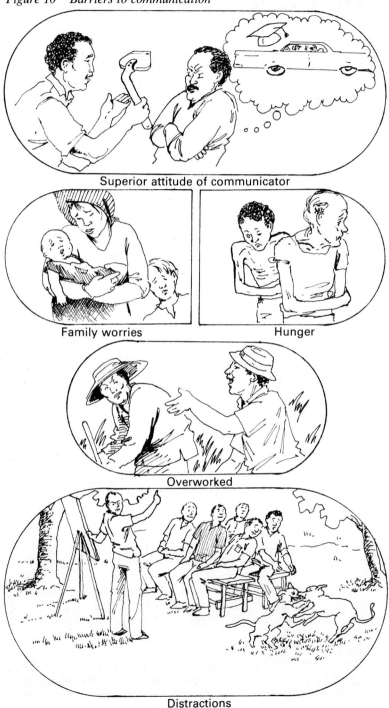

The innovation or message

A development programme will have a number of innovations which, if followed by the farmers, should increase their yields and profits or bring about other improvements to their welfare. For an innovation to be accepted by the target audience it has to have the following characteristics:

(a) *Technical correctness*

The idea must be technically correct and have been tried out under field conditions. If people try out ideas that fail, then they are unlikely to listen again to extension advice. If the risk of failure is great, the rural poor are unlikely to accept the risk.

Research work tends to be done on very complex problems and research results are not easily translatable for use by farming families.

(b) *Economic viability*

The idea must be profitable to the farmer and be sufficiently profitable to justify the changes which have to be made. In Malawi, for example, farmers were being encouraged for years by extension workers to increase their tobacco production. It was not, however, until there was a significant increase in the price offered that production increased. It actually doubled in one year.

(c) *Social and cultural acceptability*

The innovation must be generally accepted by the friends of the person who wants to try it out. People are not prepared to put themselves in a position where they may be laughed at, or where other people will disapprove of the innovation because of local custom, tradition or religious beliefs. For example, in the Gambia men were very reluctant to work in rice fields, as they regarded this as women's work. Again, in East Africa certain people will not eat fish because they think they are related to snakes.

(d) *Limited side effects*

Some innovations may create a number of problems which outweigh the benefits. For example, if encouraging a village to grow tomatoes means that another village loses a traditional market, then this is a serious side effect.

(e) *Harmony with the farming system*

The innovation should fit in with the other activities in the farming system. For example, it should not compete for too much labour at peak labour times.

(f) *Ability to be tested*

It should be possible for the farmer to try out the innovation on a limited scale before committing too much of his resources to it, or he should be able to see it demonstrated or tried by somebody else.

(g) *Available resources, supplies, spare parts*

Resources must be available so that the innovation can be taken up. Thus, for planting trees the seed or seedlings and fertilizer must be available. Or, if the use of mosquito nets is being encouraged, then they must be available locally.

Figure 11 Audience characteristics

Physical characteristics
Age
Sex
Health
Size of group

Educational characteristics
Vocabulary
Skills
Learning methods
Knowledge

Socio-economic characteristics
Culture
Economic level
Occupation
Social status

Psychological characteristics
Prejudices
Beliefs
Attitudes
Interests
Motivations

Selecting messages

A Change Agent, or the person who gives him direct support, a Subject Matter Specialist, needs to plan several months ahead what advice is likely to be needed by his farmers. When he meets the farmers, he must be prepared with the right knowledge and able to give timely demonstrations.

(a) The first step is to prepare a crop calendar. This shows all the crops in the area and what husbandry activities should occur each month. An example of a crop calendar is shown on this page.

(b) Then at monthly intervals examine the calendar and extract the monthly activities.

(c) Visit and question about 20 farmers in the area to see which activities they consider they did satisfactorily last year. Complete an 'activity analysis' form (an example is on pages 28 and 29).

(d) If a large proportion of the farmers (say, over 75 per cent) failed to do certain activities well, then these are the ones to concentrate on. Time and effort should not be wasted on activities already accepted by most of the community.

(e) Find out why a particular activity was not followed. This will affect your message. For example, if there was no fertilizer available, then make sure there will be this year and that your message says so. If, on the other hand, a crop was not planted because of a poor market price, there is little point in trying to encourage farmers to grow the crop if the price has not changed.

(f) Once you have analysed the information and decided on your message, develop the message so that it gives a positive guide. For example, it is not sufficient just to say 'spray tomatoes'. The message should be, 'In May and June spray your tomatoes weekly with Perenox. This will help to prevent them being damaged by Late Blight disease. Perenox can be purchased at the market. It costs $2 per kg and you need 4 kg per hectare.'

Example of a crop calendar

Crop	March	April	May
Rice	Prepare nursery beds.	Soak seeds. Plant in nursery.	Weed. Care of nursery.
Pineapples	Plough land. Make ridges.	Prepare planting material and plant.	Fertilize.
Tobacco	Plant nursery. Mulch.	Spray, weed and water.	Spray, weed and water.

Example of an activity analysis form
For month *May/June* Year *1983*
Crop *Cotton* Recommended practice *Spray against American bollworm*
Number of farmers covered on this form *24*. Percentage of farmers not following practice *75%*
Reasons for not following practice as given by the farmers. (Several reasons may be given.)

		tick here	total
Information	Not heard about the recommendation	✓✓✓✓✓✓✓	7
	Had too little information	✓✓✓✓	4
	Does not believe that the information is correct	✓✓	2
Marketing	Considers market prices too low	✓✓	2
	Poor market facilities	✓	1
	Difficult regulations	✓✓✓	3
Lack of inputs	Credit/money		

				7			
				3			
				✓✓✓✓✓✓			
				✓✓✓			

Labour

Water

Seed

Fertilizer

Insecticide/pesticide

Machinery

Stock

Feed

Vet/drugs

Other reasons (state)

Recommendations *for 1984. That all farmers be informed about the spraying. That chemicals be ordered well in advance.*

Self-study questions

1. What characteristics do messages require to be effective?
2. What is the use of feedback? How is it obtained?
3. What are the barriers to good communications?
4. What is the adoption process?
5. What is meant by non-verbal communication? Give examples.

Group activity study

The Innovation Game

To be played by a small group of Change Agents.

Objective
For participants to analyse a possible innovation and determine its value.

Method
Participants select two innovations currently being introduced in their area. They briefly answer in writing the questions below.

Discussion
After answering the questions, participants say whether any of the answers were negative and explain their reasons. The group discusses whether these reasons are sufficiently serious to affect the successful introduction of the innovation.

Questions	*Additional notes*
1. Do we need it? What is the size of the benefit?	It should satisfy an identified need. We should try and quantify the anticipated results, so that we can better assess its value.
2. Are there alternatives?	Is this the best available method for satisfying the need?
3. Does it pay?	There should be clear economic benefits, and these must outweigh the risks.
4. Is it socially and culturally acceptable?	Does it fit in with existing attitudes, religious practices, tenancy arrangements, etc?
5. What are the likely side effects and reactions to it?	Will it be detrimental to one group of people despite its benefits to others? (E.g., will it create unemployment?)

6. Is it technically correct?	Has the innovation been properly tested in a scientific way? Do scientists differ in their opinions about how good it is? If they do, then how can we decide who is right?
7. Do we have the resources?	Are the necessary tools, markets, supplies available, and what is their present distribution? Can they be made available if they are not already?
8. Are the right experts and field workers available?	Will extra staff be needed? Will existing staff need extra training? (Can they be trained?)
9. If it is such a good idea, why has it not been done before?	If information has been available concerning the innovation for some time, then what has been preventing its adoption? Can these 'blocking' factors be overcome?
10. Has it been done before?	What are the experiences of other groups of people using this innovation? Are their experiences relevant? (Was it used in a similar environment or not?)
11. Can we test it?	We should be able to use it on a small scale first.
12. Does it fit the farming system?	Does the average farm have the right resources, including labour? Will it interfere with present practices so that the output of other farm products suffers?
13. Who will implement this idea?	Are Change Agents to be responsible for initiating, organizing and evaluating the adoption of this innovation? Or will it be the job of local leaders, or traders?
14. What is the cost to government?	Can it be supported and promoted by existing budgets? (Are there any import–export implications?)
15. Will the market hold up?	Do past economic trends support the long term profitability of this innovation? We must be sure that there will be a future market for its products.

The Attitudes Game

Objective
>For participants to find out for themselves that attitudes to innovations vary for each audience. This will greatly affect how the message is written for each audience.

Method
>(a) Participants determine possible target groups in their own areas. These might include school children, teachers, local leaders, farmers' wives, progressive farmers, landlords, religious leaders, shopkeepers, etc.
>
>(b) List items which concern development, such as nutrition, hygiene, family planning, use of farm inputs, extension workers, police, environment, local government officials, conservation, landlords, development projects, etc.
>
>(c) Make up a grid, with the various target audiences listed along the top and the items down the side. (See the example on page 33.)
>
>(d) Divide the participants into small groups each of which fills up a column. E.g., one group will be the religious leaders, another poor farmers, and so on.
>
>(e) Participants give marks out of ten. A high mark indicates a positive attitude towards the item: they think it is a good idea. Thus 'local leaders' may give 'police' a high mark, but 'poor farmers' may give 'police' a low mark.
>
>(f) Groups enter their marks on the grid.

Conclusion
>Participants look at the marks on the grid and see that different target audiences have different attitudes. Some audiences require motivational messages, while others only need more information.
>
>It would be interesting to discuss whether the marks given also relate to the actual knowledge which audiences have about each item. In other words, does a low mark in hygiene suggest a limited knowledge of hygiene?

Examples of the grid for the Attitudes Game

Target audiences

Items concerning development	School children	Teachers	Local leaders	Farmers' wives	Progressive farmers	Poor farmers	Landlords	Religious leaders
Nutrition	8	10	6	4	7	2	5	4
Hygiene	6	10	5	4	9	2	4	4
Family planning	6	9	4	2	7	0	3	1
Farm inputs	5	8	3	2	9	1	9	4
Extension workers	4	8	5	2	6	2	10	4
Police	3	8	8	4	7	1	10	6
Environment	7	10	4	1	6	0	6	4
Etc.								

10 = most positive attitude. 0 = most negative attitude.

3 Communication methods

This chapter looks at the different ways Change Agents can work with people. The major area is working with groups, as this is considered to be the most effective in terms of staff time and costs.

Objectives

By the end of this chapter you should be able to:
   (a) State the advantages and disadvantages of using group work, individual visits and mass media.
   (b) State group needs.
   (c) Understand the different roles people take up in a group.
   (d) State the ways in which a group comes to a decision.
   (e) State the main teaching points when giving a demonstration.
   (f) Explain the difference between a result and a method demonstration.

Definitions of words used

clique	– small number of people working together
consensus	– common agreement by all
group pressure	– the influence a group can put on a member to conform to group wishes
mass media	– the various methods of transmitting messages to a large number of people
role	– the part a person takes, his task or function
task	– a job to be done

Introduction: Different communication methods

There are several ways development work can be carried out:
   (a) By individual visits.
   (b) Through the mass media.
   (c) Through traditional channels, such as story tellers, singers, puppets, mime, drama, etc.
   (d) Through village meetings.
   (e) By study visits for farmers.
   (f) By method or result demonstrations.
   (g) By working with groups.

Some comments on each method are given below. Remember, however, that all the methods are useful and the most appropriate method for the particular purpose should be carefully selected.

Individual visits

An individual visit by a Change Agent allows him to concentrate on one family's specific problems and to build up a good friendship with the family. However, the Agent's time is limited and he can only visit a few people; too often they tend to be the richer people with whom the Agent generally has more empathy. This can lead to jealousy in the community.

On a regular basis a Change Agent might visit effectively no more than four individual families a day. If he has 18 working days available per month, then the number of contacts would be 72. Most Change Agents are expected to advise over 2,000 families. By just using 'individual visits' as a method the Change Agent can only reach and work with some three to four per cent of the families.

Sometimes an Agent has to pass information quickly on to the rural population or to a section of it. Time may be a constraint and to visit personally every farmer or small village will be difficult. In addition, using trained Agents to deliver simple messages is inefficient. Change Agents make expensive postmen!

The Agent should consider who or what he can use as a cheap way of spreading information. Possible means include:

School children	– Visit the local school and ask the children to pass on the message. They will be pleased at the responsibility, and it will increase their own interest in agriculture, health, etc.
Local leaders	– Ask them to spread the word at meetings.
Farmers, Contact farmers in the T and V System	– Request their help to tell and demonstrate to their friends.
Group and local leaders	– They have the community interests at heart and will help.
Shopkeepers	– Ask them to inform their customers and to put up a notice.
Religious leaders	– People respect and listen to them.
Bulletin or notice boards	– These may be your own or belong to other organizations.
Local newsletters and magazines	– They are circulated by churches, schools, clubs, etc.
Cine film vans	– Some areas have touring commercial film vans. They might make announcements for you.

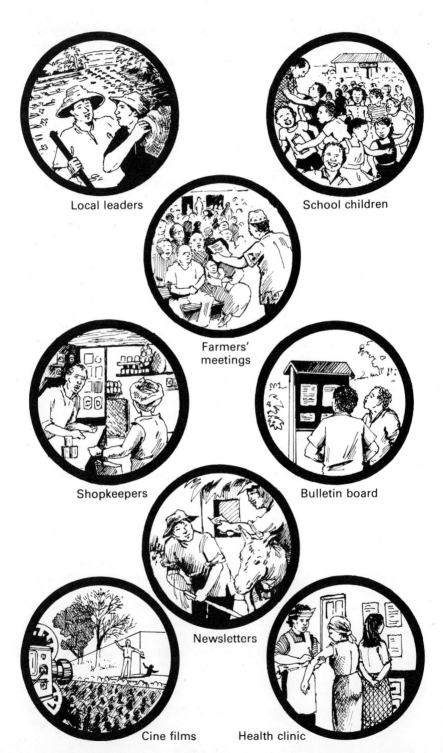

Figure 12 Local information carriers

Each Agent should build up his own channels of communication. If it is for the public good it will usually be done free. Do not forget that people like to help, they like to be involved.

Mass media

There are some important considerations to bear in mind about using the mass media:
  (a) It is the cheapest way of reaching a large number of people.
  (b) Often it is the only way of reaching isolated communities or families.
  (c) It may not be as effective as individual or group methods.
  (d) Printed media can supply a constant reference, as a person can keep a leaflet and refer to it at any time.
  (e) Radio and television can be very timely, particularly for advice on cropping, marketing and weather.
  (f) The Change Agent can have little influence on the radio and television mass media. He can, however, use them and encourage the rural community to listen to or view them.

Listening groups

In the past, considerable success has been achieved with groups of people meeting to listen to radio programmes and then discussing them (e.g., Ghana and Malawi). With more and more families in many countries now owning their own radios, this may not be so popular.

The cassette tape is being tried out in a number of countries as a means of passing information and stimulating discussion. If the message has information which needs to be remembered, then the system requires a written back-up. Recording radio programmes on to cassette tapes can be an easy way of transmitting messages. Leaders or Change Agents make the recording and replay it at more convenient times. This overcomes the considerable problem of sending out tapes to rural areas.

Some organizations are experimenting with television viewing groups (e.g., Pakistan). This may become more common, but of course only where electric power and television transmissions are available. In addition, a close relationship is needed between the television authority and the rural development organization.

There have been very interesting experiments with video film-making in countries such as Mexico and Peru. Groups of people make video films for other rural groups to show the problems they have identified and how they might solve them.

Traditional channels

These are the communication methods which have been used for centuries in rural areas, such as songs, plays, stories, puppet shows, etc. They are often neglected, though in many societies they may be the most powerful way of communicating. We have become too dependent on and influenced by so-called 'modern' methods. Our Agents and organizations must go back and examine the traditional communication methods of the country in which they work and try out traditional methods from other countries.

For example, Change Agents could write words to a popular local tune instead of making a poster. They could set up a drama or puppet show instead of showing a film. Local people or school children could be encouraged to undertake these activities.

Village meetings

Village meetings may be used to discuss problems and introduce new ideas. The meetings should be planned well in advance and involve local leaders. These meetings can lead to the formation of various groups, farmer's or women's clubs, or co-operatives.

Here is a check list for planning a meeting:
– Should the meeting be formal or informal?
– Will it be a talk, lecture or discussion?
– Who is participating, the whole village or only certain groups?
– What time?
– What place? Is it easy to reach, is it comfortable?
– What publicity is required: posters, announcements?
– Who will introduce the meeting: local leader, politician, district officer?
– What visual aids are required?
– What arrangements are needed for seating, microphones, signposts, refreshments?

Study visits for farmers

One of the best ways of interesting and motivating farmers is to arrange visits to places of interest, such as research stations, large commercial farms and to other farmers in and outside the area. When farmers talk to other farmers, the motivating influence can be much more effective than when the Change Agent is talking.

On these trips warm friendships can develop between farmers and Agents.

Demonstrations

Demonstrations usually form the backbone of informal teaching and are one of the most effective tools for a teacher in a more formal situation.

There are two types of demonstrations. The first is the *method* demonstration at which a skill or a method is shown, e.g., how to spray cotton. The second is the *result* demonstration. This shows the result of an activity over a period of time. For example, a fertilizer demonstration might consist of three separate meetings: (a) application, (b) comparing growth during the season and (c) at the harvest time.

Agents do much of their teaching by holding demonstrations. They sometimes arrange for respected local people, whose advice is sought by others, to give demonstrations. These people find that a demonstration is the best way of teaching their friends.

If you only *tell* people the best way of doing something, they will forget very quickly. People need to see something being done and then do it themselves to remember it well. A demonstration, where people take part, is the most effective way to make sure new methods are remembered.

How to give the demonstration

(a) At the start of the demonstration tell your audience what you are trying to teach them and how it can help them.

(b) Make sure everybody can see and hear well. Everybody will be able to see if they all stand well back.

(c) Do not run your demonstrations with people standing for a long time in the hot sun.

(d) Talk *with* your audience, do not talk *at* them, and do not talk too much.

(e) Each person should take a part in the demonstration, so make sure everybody tries their hand. Get the audience to ask questions, and ask them questions to make sure they are following you. Remember, if the audience takes part, the demonstration will be a success.

(f) Watch out for the slow learners and give them extra help. Repeat the steps of the demonstration if necessary.

(g) If you do not know an answer, say 'I do not know, but I will find out'. Find the answer later, then get in touch with the questioner and inform him of the answer.

Important points

(a) Teach each method at the correct time of the year, e.g., teach how to plant groundnuts just before the farmers should be planting.

(b) Be realistic. Do not teach farmers about chemicals they cannot obtain, or about the use of machines they cannot afford.

(c) Plan ahead. Make sure your meeting does not clash with other meetings.

(d) Make sure everything is ready the day before the demonstration.

(e) Give plenty of advance notice of the meeting.

From a cost-effective viewpoint, working with groups is probably the best method for the Change Agent. How to go about this is considered next.

Figure 13   Giving a demonstration

Group work

Group work is very much cheaper than individual visits. The Agent's time is limited; therefore working with groups is likely to be more cost-effective.

'Group pressure' can be most effective on those doubters who are not easily convinced of the value of the innovation. Members of a group can have a stronger influence on each other than the Agent can.

People in groups can more easily share experiences.

How groups operate

Every group of people has two basic characteristics: it has a task to undertake and it has to maintain itself as a group.

A group is formed because some people have a similar problem or need and by working as a group they will best be able to solve it. This is the group's 'task need'. The group may be formed to prevent something happening, such as the building of a factory in a residential area, or to undertake something, such as forming a marketing outlet for produce. (The group is more likely to stay together while the task is being accomplished, because everyone then has a common goal.)

Once the task has been completed, and unless a new one is found, the group will distintegrate. During the task period the group leader will have to try to keep the group together. This is called 'group maintenance'.

What motivates people?
Do they want:
    to be more beautiful?
    to be stronger?
    to be healthier?
    to have more prestige?
    to have more free time?
    to have more money?
Which are most important?

Figure 14 Motivation

Roles of group members

Members normally each play a role that helps the group come to a decision. These roles are adopted naturally, according to personality; but an Agent himself may have to play certain roles, if they are lacking in the group, for it to perform efficiently.

The positive roles are:
(a) Initiator/contributor: one who seeks new ideas.
(b) Information seeker: asks for factual clarification.
(c) Opinion seeker: asks for opinions of others.
(d) Information giver: offers 'authoritative' facts.
(e) Elaborator: spells out suggestions in terms of examples and describes how an idea would work in practice.

(f) Co-ordinator: tries to pull ideas together.
(g) Orientator: defines positions with respect to group goals.
(h) Evaluator/critic: evaluates group performance.
(i) Energizer: prods the group into action.
(j) Procedural technician: speeds up group action by handling routine arrangements like setting up projectors or arranging seating.
(k) Recorder: notes suggestions, group decisions or results of discussion.

Group members may also play negative roles that threaten the efficiency of the group and are often hard to control. Group pressure may be necessary to control them. Typical negative roles include:

(a) Aggressor: may criticize others; express disapproval of values, acts or feelings of others; may joke aggressively.

(b) Playboy: may be casual, nonchalant, and generally display a lack of involvement in the group.

(c) Dominator: tries to assert authority or superiority by manipulating the group or certain members of it. He may frequently interrupt the contributions of others.

(d) Blocker: maintains a negative attitude and is stubborn. He disagrees beyond reason and attempts to bring back the issue after the group has rejected it.

The agent should be able to identify all these roles within a group and should try to encourage other group members to control these people.

The group leader's role

In group discussions, the Change Agent should guide the group leader to:

(a) Build upon common experiences and understandings.
There are likely to be members in the group who have specific knowledge of the task.

(b) Clarify procedures.
Determine how the discussion will be conducted, in what order, what it will seek to accomplish and when it will conclude.

(c) Restrict the discussion topic.
Make sure that it can be discussed in the time allotted.

(d) Allow the discussion to move away from its planned course.
There are times when such a step promises to be fruitful.

(e) Build up a spirit of group co-operation and friendliness.
Discourage taking sides on an issue.

(f) Ask questions which demand facts and opinions.
Discourage questions which can be answered with a yes or no.

(g) Avoid playing a too dominant role in the discussions.
Put the responsibility on the participants. Throw back questions to the group; do not answer them yourself, ask group members to respond to statements of other members.

(h) Summarize from time to time.

Figure 15 Group pressure

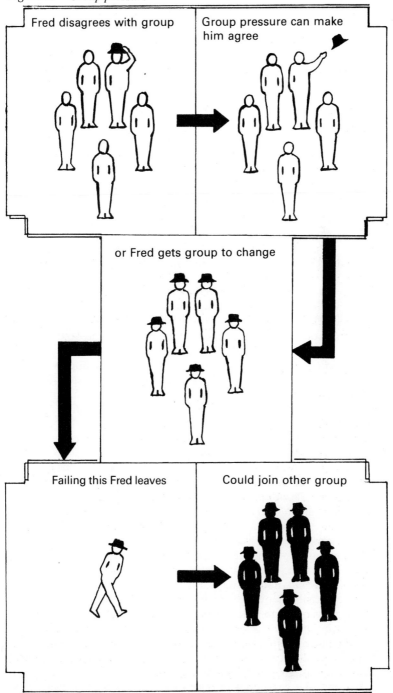

Remind the group of its progress, its unfilfilled commitments, and its remaining time.

(i) Restate and clarify contributions when necessary.

Align contributions with the discussion. Ask participants for illustrative examples or restatements so that meanings become clearer.

(j) Recognize varying opinions or options.

On any problem under discussion there may be several. Help to formulate these.

(k) Leave time for a summary.

This should be done by one or more participants serving as recorder.

How a group reaches a decision

The group leader and the Change Agent should be aware of how decisions are made. They should try and guide the group to making a consensus decision, so as to maintain and strengthen the group.

The one-person decision. This is quickly made. But the decision maker depends on the free or voluntary support of others to implement the decision or else he may find himself carrying it out alone.

The handclasp. One person makes a suggestion, another says 'what a marvellous idea' and, without further discussion, the matter is decided. These decisions occur more frequently than you think and often pass unnoticed at the time. But resentment comes to the surface later.

The clique. A decision is made by a small group who plan beforehand to have their own way. Because they are better organized than those who might disagree, they are often successful on the immediate issue, but they bring a spirit of rivalry rather than co-operation into the group.

Unpopular suggestions. Here the group makes a decision by not making a decision. 'Not to decide – is to decide.' Someone makes a suggestion, but it drops like a stone into a pond, and no one pays any attention to it. If the person who made the suggestion really felt enthusiastic about it, the fact that it was totally ignored could either make the person withdraw or resist later suggestions.

Minority. These decisions are not as consciously organized as those of the clique. A few powerful personalities dominate the group, often unconsciously, and then they wonder why the others lack enthusiasm later.

Majority vote. In big groups this is often the most effective way to make a decision. However, the group may lose the interest or loyalty of the minority who voted against a decision, especially if they feel their point of view has not been given a fair hearing.

Consensus. This is an agreement (often involving compromise or the combination of various possibilities) after all opinions have been heard and disagreements and minority viewpoints discussed fully. It takes time and care to encourage a climate in which all feel free to express themselves. It means adapting the decision to accommodate the concerns of all. It may take longer to make a decision this way, but it will be carried out more quickly and wholeheartedly.

To have a true consensus you should:
– Agree beforehand on the method of discussion.
– Have an understanding on how the group will make its decision.
– Have good ways of stimulating the discussion and sharing ideas.

Self-study questions

1. Compare the effectiveness of individual visits and mass media in extension work.
2. List the important considerations to be made while planning a demonstration.
3. State the advantages and disadvantages of groups in development work.
4. State some of the qualities of an effective group leader.
5. How do the attitudes of individuals, the attitude of the group and the attitude of the leader significantly affect the group process and the success of the group in reaching a decision?

Group decision making

Objective
To study how a group functions.

Method
Choose a group of five people. The remaining people act as observers. Ask the trainees to discuss a controversial subject such as: 'What is the value of radio in development work?' or 'Rural people do not need to be literate'. Keep the time short (10–15 minutes). Emphasize that the group must come to a decision.

Do not appoint a chairman, secretary, etc. Let the group sort themselves out. Watch the group in action and note the steps taken by the group and the interaction between people.

Conclusion
Did the group fail to come to a decision because:
– It was concentrating on giving opinions, asking for opinions, explaining and clarifying, rather than evaluating facts.
– It had no agreement on a common goal.
– There was no clear analysis of the problem.
– There was a struggle between a few, the others were withdrawn and not involved.

Studying group activity

A good way to learn how to work with groups is to watch one in action. To help you study the group critically, use the evaluation form on page 46. Where did the group do well and where did it fail?

		Poor	Fair	Average	Good	Excellent
Group evaluation form		1	2	3	4	5
1. Preparation	How satisfactory were the 'physical' preparations (accommodation, materials, etc.)?					
2. Opening	Did the discussion get off to a good start?					
3. Objective	Was the general purpose of the meeting clearly stated?					
4. Topic	Was the topic announced clearly and concisely? Was it introduced well?					
5. Atmosphere	Was there a relaxed, friendly atmosphere?					
6. Participation	Did the leader encourage all-round participation?					
7. Keeping to the subject	How well did the leader manage to keep the discussion on the announced topic?					
8. Questions	Were they well designed? Were they well distributed around the group? Did they stimulate discussion?					
9. Leader's own contribution	Was the leader careful not to pose as an expert?					
10. Pace of discussion	Did the discussion keep moving and making progress?					
11. Control of group	How well did the leader control personal arguments, private chats, irrelevant material?					
12. Intermediate summaries	Did the leader make adequate intermediate summaries?					
13. Visual presentation	Was it well planned? Was it well executed?					
14. Final summary	How adequate was the final summary?					
15. Closure	How adequate was the closure?					
16. Achievement of objective	Was the objective of the meeting achieved?					

4 Using audio-visual aids

The reasons for the importance of audio-visual aids in teaching and extension work are discussed in this chapter. It covers what media can be used, particularly low cost media, and how the appropriate media should be selected. Some suggestions about how to use audio-visual aids when teaching are included, as well as information on design, construction and writing. The care and operation of audio-visual equipment are covered.

Objectives

By the end of this chapter you should be able to:
 (a) Name the various audio-visual aids which are likely to be useful in extension work.
 (b) Explain how audio-visual aids can help extension work and teaching.
 (c) Select audio-visual aids appropriate to the needs of your audience and according to the resources available.
 (d) Design and construct certain audio-visual aids.
 (e) Keep audio-visual equipment in good working order.

Definitions of words used

audio-visual aid	– in this book refers to an instrument or learning material which can be seen and heard, or just seen or just heard
channel	– the object or thing through which a message is transmitted (e.g., newspapers, films, radio, posters)
communication	– the transfer of information (including ideas, emotions, knowledge, skills, etc.) from person to person
edit	– to check communications material, removing or changing parts of the material, or suggesting additions
hardware	– the machinery or equipment, especially electrical, electronic, optical, used to transmit and receive messages (e.g., cameras, projectors, typewriters, radio transmitters and receivers)

medium (plural 'media')	– any object or system used for, or capable of, transmitting messages (e.g., film, poster, leaflet, radio)
pre-test	– to try out a communication with just a sample from the target audience
proof-read	– to read written material in order to correct grammar, spelling and punctuation
software	– the message or content of a communication, or the more 'consumable' media, which carry the message (e.g., books, posters, slides, films, tapes)
video-tape	– a reel of tape on which can be recorded both sound and pictures. It can then be played through a television set.

Introduction: Communications media

Communications media are used by organizations or individuals to convey messages. These messages might be to individuals or to large audiences. The information can be timely and the cost relatively cheap per person contacted. Communications media are normally used in programmes to support the Agent's efforts, by reinforcing the Agent's messages or reaching audiences he cannot reach.

As part of their training, Change Agents should know how to operate all the media equipment which could be useful to them. Even more important, Agents should receive training in producing low cost media. Then some media will always be available and, having been produced locally, will be more appropriate to the community. The Agent will need the support of his organization, as materials for producing media may be difficult for him to obtain by himself.

Advantages and disadvantages of media

Some extension situations may require a personal visit to a farmer. The cost of an individual visit is high and organizations are now concentrating on group visits backed up by media.

Communications media

Advantages	Disadvantages
Can reach large audiences.	The cost of equipment is initially high.
Relatively inexpensive per person reached.	Maintenance and repairs may be expensive and difficult.
Can reach the isolated.	Not easy to obtain good feedback from the audience.
Only a small staff required.	
Can give out timely news.	
Can reach people every day in their own homes.	

Personal visits

Advantages
Personal contact can sometimes be very effective in motivating farmers. Good feedback can be obtained.

Disadvantages
Visits to farmers can be very expensive, and can only be done at intervals. Often only the more advanced farmers are visited. Many staff are required to give good coverage.

Every personal visit should always be backed up by using communications media as it makes them more cost-effective. However, as farmers become more motivated and as the communications media improve, face-to-face communications can be reduced. In situations where the farming community is well-motivated, the use of media alone is effective.

Sometimes farming people rely almost exclusively on media for their information. The radio or television gives them weather or market news and also information about outbreaks of insect pests. The commercial media inform them of good buys in machinery, fertilizer, stock, seed, buildings, etc. The farming press and magazines provide more detailed information and articles about farming enterprises. The radio may even broadcast farm family serial programmes which creates interest and may provide some knowledge and motivation.

Relative effectiveness of various aids

Visual media are particularly important, since research suggests that most of what we learn is through our eyes, rather than through our ears, touch or sense of smell. Thus, as the Chinese apparently said, one picture is worth a thousand words.

What people remember some days after being presented with a message is much more important than what they recall immediately afterwards. Research shows that a combination of words and visuals after a three day time lapse is some six times more effective than just words

	Recall after 3 hours	Recall after 3 days
words only	70%	10%
visuals only	72%	20%
words and visuals	85%	65%

The theoretical effectiveness of various learning aids is shown in Figure 16 on page 50. The real experience is most effective, followed by viewing, while the spoken word tends to be least effective. Yet, in spite of these facts, much of our teaching and extension is still done by lecture and talk.

Figure 16 Theoretical effectiveness of various aids in learning

Most effective
—— Practical work
—— Demonstration
—— Television or slides
—— Still pictures
—— Books and print
—— Lecture

Least effective

The quality of the teaching, of course, is of vital importance; for example, an interesting lecture may be more effective than a poorly run demonstration.

Teaching with audio-visual aids

(a) Film, video-tape and television

The importance of television as a teaching and motivating medium was understated at first. People now realize, however, that it is a very powerful medium, not only for teaching and imparting information, but also in changing attitudes. In some countries many families watch as much as six hours of television each day. For many younger people it is their main source of information and ideas. Thus, where television is available, it is sensible to use it to communicate good ideas about development to the rural community.

A television programme can form an excellent base for a lesson or discussion, as can showing a film or running a video-tape. The advantage of video-tape and film over television is that they can be stopped at intervals to discuss what has happened so far.

(b) Overhead transparencies

Teachers can make their own transparencies for display on an overhead projector. Colourful, well thought-out transparencies can greatly improve a lesson. The teacher remains seated, facing the

Figure 17 Using overhead projector

class, and time is not wasted in drawing on the blackboard. Another great advantage is that overhead transparencies can be stored for future lessons.

(c) Slides

Good quality cameras can be purchased by the extension organization and are relatively inexpensive nowadays as is slide processing. So showing slides is a good option in training.

The Change Agent usually needs guidance on planning a sequence of slides to tell a story and on taking good technical slides. Too many photos are taken from too great a distance and with too many people in the picture. The best photos are carefully posed with just one person in the picture: the main interest is the process and equipment being used.

Figure 18   Example of good slide series

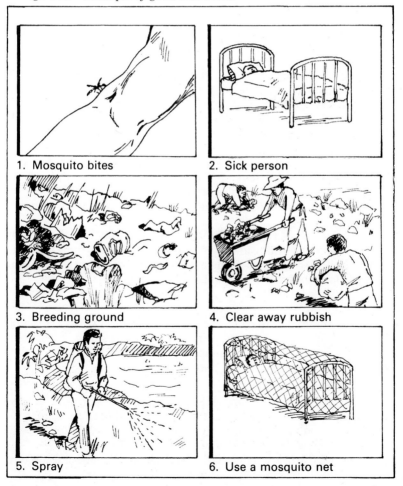

Once the slide set is complete, you can write a script for the teacher to read aloud or you can record it on tape, though this loses the personal touch. Again, the real benefit is that the slides can be used many times.

With slides, films and television, the major problems are the initial cost of equipment, the difficulty of maintaining it and obtaining spares. But cheaper visuals exist, which can be fully under the control of the teacher or Change Agent.

(d) Writing boards

Blackboards or chalk boards are simple but very useful teaching aids. There is also another type of board made of white plastic for which special pens are required.

The following points will help you to use a chalk board more effectively.

1. *Minimizing glare*

When positioning a chalk board, view it from several parts of the room to make sure there is no glare. Place the board at an angle to the audience if necessary.

Before using a new chalk board, its surface should be lightly rubbed over with chalk dust. An old chalk board eraser can be used. This treatment will prevent permanent marks being left when the board is used for the first time.

When old boards become shiny they are of little use, as the chalk will not make clearly visible marks. Such boards should be repainted.

2. *Using the board*

When writing on the board, words with separated letters are easier to read than normal writing, and with practice they can be nearly as quick to write. Non-capitals are easier to read than capitals because of the variations in the height of the letters, which assist quick recognition.

To find out the right size for your writing, check from the back of the classroom. Writing in straight lines is a problem to some teachers. This can be solved by walking as you write, or you can draw a thin line beforehand to act as a guide.

(e) Flannelgraphs

Flannelgraphs consist of a rough-textured cloth, such as a blanket or piece of felt, on to which drawings, photographs or words can be placed. The drawings have sandpaper glued to the back which makes them stick to the fluff of the cloth.

1. *Advantages*

– You can build up a story by placing the symbols or words on the flannelgraph in a planned sequence. (This should be rehearsed.)

– The symbols can be re-used.

– Flannelgraphs are easy and inexpensive to make.

– They need little storage space as the cloth can be rolled or folded up. Alternatively a blanket can be borrowed for the show.

Figure 19   Using real objects for teaching

- The presentation can be more colourful and interesting than with a blackboard.

2. *Disadvantages*
- When used outside, the wind can blow the symbols off the cloth.
- You need suitable publications from which to cut out the illustrations, or some artistic skill to draw your own.

3. *Points to watch when using*
- Explain how it works before starting, so that people do not spend all the time wondering about it.
- Pre-test the pictures before using them.
- Do not stand between the flannelgraph and the audience.
- Rehearse your presentation.
- Do not clutter up the flannelgraph with too many pictures.

(f) Real objects

The best visual aid is the real object and this should be used whenever possible. The audience should be allowed to see and feel the object, e.g., seeds, fertilizer, a piece of equipment, etc.

Specimens can be placed in bottles. This is particularly useful with pests and diseases, so that farmers can recognize them. Grasses and plant samples can be dried and pressed by putting them between absorbent paper under a brick. After a few days they can be stuck on to a piece of cardboard with Sellotape.

Samples should be small enough to be easily transported.

(g) Models

Models are useful when describing buildings, such as dairy parlours, or discussing soil conservation or how machines work, but they do require a lot of effort to make. They are more often used in exhibitions. The scale of the model should be shown, and you must make sure that things which are small in reality are not made too large on the model. If they are out of proportion, they may not easily be recognized. Models are very useful for teaching audiences with a mixture of knowledge or education, as they can be understood by everyone.

(h) Flip chart

A flip chart is a series of pictures, each on a separate page, which are fastened together at the top. They are shown one by one to illustrate a story or message. Therefore, the pictures should be in a planned sequence so that a story unfolds as each page is turned.

The advantages are that flip charts are cheap and easy to make, they can be small and thus easy to carry, and they do not blow away in the wind like flannelgraph pictures do.

(i) Flash cards

These are large pieces of card with a picture or a few words written on each of them. They are used to emphasize important points during a lecture. They should be quite large, and each should be displayed at the relevant point of the lecture.

(j) Newsprint pads (unprinted newspaper)

Newsprint is quite cheap to obtain and, when coloured markers are used on it, it can be an attractive teaching aid. It will probably have to be obtained by the organization.

(k) Glove puppets

A puppet is a small doll characterizing a person or an animal. They are used as actors in short plays or dramas and have been used very successfully in many countries. Puppets are especially useful as a teaching aid when the level of literacy is low, or where people are traditionally interested in story and drama. A close and intimate relationship can be built up between the puppets and members of the audience.

A puppet story can be made up about local problems and a puppet can have a discussion with a member of the audience. Also, puppets can be outrageous and say things to an audience that would be offensive in some societies if said by the Change Agent; for example, comments on hygiene, latrines, or birth control.

Puppets can be made from papier-maché, Polyfilla, wood, cloth stuffed with kapok, etc. The simplest puppets are glove puppets, the controlling hand being concealed by the puppet's clothes.

(l) Displays

If you have an extension office, a farm club, or a local co-operative building, then set up a display to attract interest in an extension topic. Your display could include samples of leaflets, posters and magazines available to farmers. Samples of weeds, pests, diseased plant material with recommendations for treatment could also be displayed, and new equipment and seeds of a new variety.

The display should be changed every few months to create new interest.

(m) Posters

Posters are useful to remind people of a message. They should be kept simple with just one message. The poster can also be used to announce a meeting. A poster for this purpose should clearly state the purpose, place, date and time. Posters have to gain the attention of the passer-by and therefore need to be attractive, colourful and cheap.

As people in rural areas are not usually in such a hurry as in urban areas, it is perhaps possible to include more information on a poster intended for them than for an urban poster. A poster, for example, may say 'Use fertilizer for good crops'. Other information could be included about what crops to use it on, how much is needed, where to buy it and the cost.

(n) Wall charts

Wall charts are used for teaching purposes or to supply extra information or reference material. They would normally be placed in a position where they could be discussed or explained, such as a classroom or a farmer's club. Such charts can show a process of sequence of events.

People have time to study the wall charts and so there can be a number of messages or ideas on each chart. They are thus quite different from posters.

Medium selection

The question is frequently asked 'What is the most effective medium for teaching?' This is rather like asking 'What is the best method of transport?', where the answer depends on where you want to go and how much money you have. In other words, there is no medium which is the best for all circumstances, there are simply appropriate media for each circumstance.

You should realize that the target audience and the message come first. Once these are decided then the selection of the most appropriate media can be undertaken.

So, 'The message before the medium'.

Multiple use of a message

Once the target audience has been selected and the message written, consideration should be given to using a number of channels for the same message. This greatly reinforces the impact, as the audience hears it from a number of sources and the 'creative effort' of producing the initial message can be exploited several times. Thus, for example, a message about cotton spraying could be carried on the radio, in a leaflet, on a poster and a flip chart. The same principle applies to drawings, thus saving time on graphics, and again reinforcing the message because of the repetition.

The production process

The steps to follow when producing any of the above visual aids are:
   (a) Think carefully about:
1. what you message is,
2. who your audience is,
3. where it will be used, and
4. what resources are available (including time).

   (b) Write the message in clear simple language. The visuals should also be clear and relevant to the message. Remove any unnecessary items from the drawings or photographs.
   (c) Design layout.
   (d) Test the draft on a few of the target audience (page 61).
   (e) Revise the draft using your pre-test results.

Aids to drawing

If you think that you cannot draw, then there are some other techniques to use:

(a) *Photographs and illustrations*

Use photographs and illustrations from newspapers, company advertisements, tin labels, etc. Cut them out and stick them on the poster. These pictures can be outlined to make them clearer.

(b) *Tracing*

Using thin paper, place it over the picture which you want to copy. You should be able to see the picture through the paper. This will enable you to copy it easily. If you cannot see through the paper, then place both the picture and the paper on a window. The picture will show up more clearly because of the light shining through it.

(c) *Templates*

Templates are shapes cut out of plywood or stout cardboard around which the teacher draws the outline. This will enable you to do a quick and satisfactory drawing of an object which normally is difficult to draw. Templates are only worth making if you are likely to use them several times.

(d) *Stencils* (for blackboards)

These can be made by punching large holes in a piece of strong paper on which the drawing has been made. The holes are positioned at the important angles of the drawing. The paper is then held against the board and patted with a chalky eraser. Take the paper away and dots will remain. Then join up the dots. Stencils and templates can be used many times over.

(e) *Enlarging*

Draw equal sized squares over the picture you want to copy. Then, on

Figure 20 Enlarging

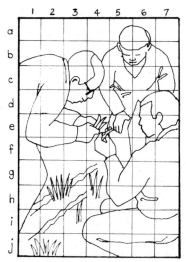

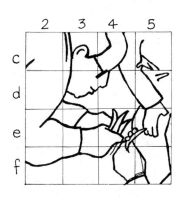

a larger piece of paper, draw the same number of squares but with bigger spaces between the lines. Copy the drawing, square by square.

(f) *Copying a photographic slide*

Project the slide on to a piece of paper fastened to a wall. Move the projector backward and forward until you project an image of the size you want. Draw an outline around the objects in the projected picture.

Points to watch when designing visual aids

– Lettering should be bold and simple.
– Strong colours should be used.
– Avoid unnecessary detail and decoration.
– Full figure drawings of animals or persons should be used. Where, for example, a close-up of hands holding something is required, show two pictures: firstly, one of the person, then the close-up picture of the hands. (See Figure 21.)
– Social customs and traditions must be correctly portrayed.

Figure 21   Showing figure then the detail

Production of written materials

Extension leaflets may be available at your department headquarters, and you should try to keep a stock available for your audience. But in any case if you have a photocopier or a duplicator, then a simple leaflet which you have written yourself can easily be produced. It could then be given out at the end of a demonstration or to individual farmers seeking information.

In many areas illiteracy is a problem, although often a farmer's children may be able to read the leaflet to him. It may thus be misleading to say a community is only ten per cent literate, if the ten per cent reads to the others.

You must consider the target audience and the message before you start to write. You must be quite clear who you are writing to and what you are really trying to say. (See Chapter 2, 'Target audiences' and 'The innovation or message', pages 23–25.)

Writing style

Before writing a leaflet or article you must plan the order of the content and how you will make it interesting. Where will the main argument be placed? Where will the educational matter or technical part be? Is it to be entertaining, informative, or argumentative?

Use simple language, which means:
– Use short sentences.
– Use familiar words which people understand.
– Use precise words with positive meanings, not words like 'generally, few, nearly, frequently'.
– Use repetition to reinforce the message.
– Use positive sentences, not negative ones.
– Stress that the message is intended for your audience by using words like 'you' and 'here'.
– Do not miss out connecting words like 'the' and 'a'. You are not writing a telegram.
– Explain logically and in the correct time sequence.
– Consider using a question-and-answer technique.
– Break up the text by using short paragraphs and drawings.
– Use visuals rather than words when possible.

Editing

Editing is the process of correcting and modifying a script. It is not a good idea to edit your own work. You need a fresh unbiased person to do this. All written material should be edited so that mistakes can be caught in time. No writer should resent editing.

Editing involves:
– Checking the script for technical accuracy.
– Ensuring that the level of writing matches the education of the target audience.
– Deciding on whether too little or too much material has been included. Sometimes non-essential information merely confuses the reader.
– Rewriting when the language is confusing, boring and repetitive.
– Dealing tactfully with writers and obtaining approval from them for corrections and changes made.

Proof reading

This consists of checking the grammar and spelling and ensuring that nothing has been left out by the typist. Proof reading must be done before finally printing or duplicating your leaflet.

Pre-testing audio-visual materials

There are two reasons why pre-testing is very important. The first is that you must know whether your message is understood and accepted by your audience. The second reason is that production of audio-visual aids is expensive, and if aids are produced which people do not understand, then money will have been wasted. In addition, you will have lost credibility with your audience.

Pre-testing attempts to find out:

(a) if the mesage is attractive so that people will want to see or read it, and how it could be made more attractive;

(b) whether the target audience understands or comprehends it and how it should be altered;

(c) whether the target audience accepts the idea in the message, or the reasons why it does not accept the idea.

It is essential to pre-test all messages you send, so that they can be amended to ensure the audience receives the meaning you intend. In the past too much emphasis, perhaps, has been given by communication researchers to those who are graphically illiterate. Most farmers can easily understand good drawings or good photographs. However, sometimes the artist has not produced a clear drawing, or the words convey a different meaning to the reader. This problem occurs quite frequently, as the writers and artists often live in a different environment and have a different educational background. Their attitudes and use of certain words are likely to be different from those of the average farm family.

An organization may employ a person as a media evaluator to test messages and give guidance to writers and artists. However, he should not undertake the evaluation of messages without closely collaborating with the message creators. They should be the chief people doing the testing, for they will find out how to improve their productions. If they are left out of the testing process, then conflict between the evaluator and the message creators will almost certainly occur.

We are not concerned with highly elaborate scientific testing. Our aim is to improve the comprehension of the message by the target audience to an acceptable level, for example, from 50 to 70 per cent. We are not aiming at 100 per cent, and it may be that if this was achieved the message would be very boring! Although understood by everyone, it would attract little attention.

Research has shown that some of the rural population also find difficulty in understanding pictures, because they may not recognize something in the picture. These people have had little exposure to pictures and little experience of interpreting them. With more exposure this changes quite quickly. Formally educated people will have been exposed to pictures at school and have developed the skill of interpreting them.

Here are two case studies that emphasize the need for pre-testing.

An agricultural Change Agent gave a demonstration in which he used a drawing to show how to transplant coffee trees. When he visited the farmers a few months later, he discovered that they had transplanted their trees, but that the nearest trees were bigger and farther apart than those behind them. This was because they had followed the drawing, where perspective had made the trees look smaller and close together when they were farther away.

In another situation, a health worker showed a film on how mosquitoes carry disease. During the film there were a number of close-up pictures of mosquitoes. After the film, the health worker was told that local people did not have this problem because the mosquitoes in this area were a lot smaller than those in the film.

The lesson to be learnt is that your audience may easily misunderstand what seems very clear to you. Pre-testing is a way of overcoming this problem.

Doing the pre-test

(a) Introduce yourself to the chosen sample of your audience. Explain that you would like them to answer some questions about the pictures you have. You must give people the feeling that you are really interested in their views.

(b) Ask about each part of the picture separately. Do not laugh if people give strange answers.

(c) Do not ask leading questions, e.g., 'Is this a cow?' Instead ask 'What do you think this is?' or 'What do you see in this picture?'

(d) If someone replies vaguely, press for a more definite answer, e.g., 'What is this?' 'An animal.' 'What sort of an animal do you think it is?' 'A cow.' Once you have a definite answer, even a wrong one, go on to the next part.

(e) Ask what people think the whole picture is trying to say (what is the message?), e.g., 'What do you think the whole picture is trying to tell you?' or 'Is this picture trying to tell you anything?'

(f) Record the answers on your response sheet.

(g) Also ask how much schooling your test audience has had. This will help you to decide if their opinion is representative of the target audience. Ask them if they have any suggestions for improving the visual aid. You will get some excellent suggestions from some of your audience, and these are important as merely to know that the picture is unsatisfactory is not very helpful.

When testing

(a) Divide the visual aid into parts, testing each part separately.

To do this you may need to hide parts of the poster, or make separate drafts.

(b) Number each part you are going to test.

(c) Produce a response sheet for recording people's comments (see below).

Name	Approx. age	Sex	Number of years of education	What does the picture show?	What does the writing show?	Suggestion for improvement

Operation, care and maintenance of equipment

16 mm sound projector

Projectors vary in design according to the companies that make them. It is therefore important to study the operation manual for your projector, to know the correct instructions on how it should be used and looked after. However, all projectors have some basic similarities in care and operation.

Care and maintenance

Clean the lens regularly with a soft camelhair lens brush. More resistant marks can be removed with lens tissue or a piece of soft non-fluffy material and lens cleansing fluid.

Condenser lenses should be removed and cleaned periodically, but care must be taken to replace them correctly. Never touch the lens with your fingers, as this leaves a grease deposit.

Remove all dust along the film-path using a suitable brush. Dust often accumulates at the film-gate and in the optical sound system. Dust will scratch the film.

When not in use, store projectors in a cupboard or cover with polythene.

Operating projectors

(a) Prepare the room and projector before the session begins.

(b) Check the film for breaks.

(c) Load the film properly, according to the manual.

(d) Check the sound quality and volume. Make any necessary adjustments. The loudspeaker should be pointed at the centre of the audience and should be at the side of the screen, not behind it, but close to the picture.

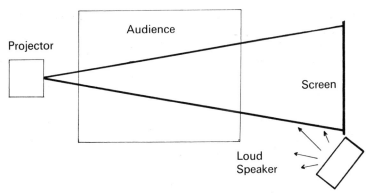

Figure 22   Positioning of loudspeaker

(e) The film title should be in the gate. Do not start with the run-in numbers on the film leader as this is not professional. Set up before the lesson.

(f) The film projector should be correctly focused. Screens often have a black edge. For a clearly defined picture the projected film should fill the screen area so that it is slightly overlapping the black edge.

(g) The various cables must be clear of the gangways and fixed safely.

(h) The projector light beam must be arranged so that the heads of the audience will not get in the way.

(i) A clear view of the screen is obtained by elevating it (too much elevation is uncomfortable). Do not place seats one behind another, as this blocks the view of the person behind.

Commentary

Each film should be introduced by the organizer to enable the audience to have an early grasp of the subject. If a discussion is to follow a film, tell the audience beforehand, so that they may note particular points of interest.

Slide projector

The preparation and management of a slide show is very similar to that of a 16 mm film presentation. Some extra points to bear in mind are:

– If the cooling blower stops working, switch the projector off immediately, otherwise the bulb will explode.

– Make sure the slides are put into the projector the correct way round. It becomes easier if slides are marked by a spot or number near where they are held by the thumb of the right hand.

– The commentary should flow naturally and easily. Voice expression is important, because gestures will not be visible. It is a good idea to rehearse the commentary. You do not need to talk all the time.

Overhead projector

This is an important teaching aid. About the only thing that can go wrong with it is that the bulb may explode, so always keep one spare.

Overhead transparencies can be prepared on clear plastic by using the correct marker pens.

Use of a microphone

Microphones are very delicate and sensitive pieces of equipment and are often misused. To avoid damage and to obtain high quality sound there are three rules:

(a) Never blow into or tap a microphone. This action causes serious damage. To test whether a microphone is on just click your fingers, or say 'testing 1, 2, 3'.

(b) Most microphones should be held at 30–45 centimetres in front of the mouth. Holding it closer than this distorts the voice.

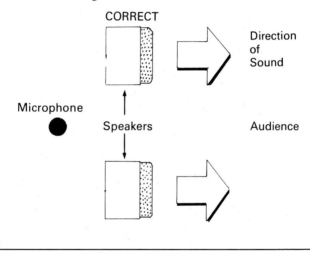

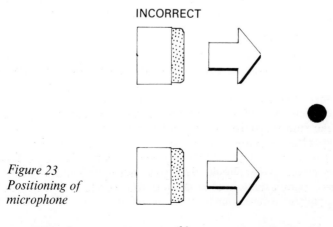

Figure 23
Positioning of microphone

(c) The loudspeaker should not be aimed at the microphone. This causes the screeching noise so often heard. For best results place the loudspeakers so that they point away from the microphone.

Tape-recorder

Tape-recorders are used quite widely in extension work, now that they have become cheaper.

Operation and care
This varies with the make of the tape-recorder and you should follow the instruction manual provided. However, all tape-recorders are damaged by dust and so should be kept clean. Tapes should be kept in dust-proof containers, away from excesses of temperature and humidity. Do not leave tapes on, or very near electric motors, radios, speakers or amplifiers as the magnetic field may spoil the recording on the tape.

Recording
Some general points:
– Use a room that is quiet.
– Do not place the microphone on the same table as the recorder, otherwise it will pick up the motor noise, which will then be recorded.
– Do not handle the microphone during a recording as this also causes noises.
– When recording with a group of people around a table, place the microphone on a soft cushion to insulate it from the sounds of paper being moved on the table.
– When outside in windy conditions, the microphone should be shielded to prevent sound interference from the wind.
– Recordings can be improved if a sound-absorbent backing is provided, e.g., opening a large book and placing it behind the microphone, or covering a chair with a blanket and placing a microphone on it.
– A simple recording booth can be made by draping a blanket over a pole which has been fixed across the corner of a room.

Self-study questions

1. What is the importance of visual aids in the work of the Change Agent?
2. Explain the main considerations in selecting media.
3. Compare wallcharts and flannelgraphs and discuss which you think are most effective, when and why.
4. Design a poster and a flip chart.
5. (a) Explain the need for pre-testing and how it should be done.
   (b) Pre-test some of your own visual aids in the field, with a small group of people from your target audience. Also test a professionally made poster.

6. What changes should be made in the light of your findings?
7. Make puppets and write a simple script for a puppet play.
8. Why is an overhead projector a useful teaching aid?

Group activity studies

Printed Communications Judgement Game

Objective
This game aims to give people the ability to judge logically the quality and suitability of printed communications. Many people will like or dislike a particular leaflet but be unable to analyse why.

Organization
The materials required are about ten different samples of printed communication material. The game should be played by 10–15 people. If more people are involved you will require several samples of each printed example.
Participants should judge each sample on paper quality, cover, binding, printing quality, clarity of layout, attractiveness, suitability for audience.

Discussion
Have participants decide which are the best samples, then have them justify their choices.

Slide Judgement Game

Objective
For participants to understand what makes a good slide.

Organization
Choose 20 slides of varied quality. Show these to the participants several times. Each participant records his opinion of each slide and gives reasons.

Discussion
Discuss the individual findings. Participants should appreciate that a good technical slide is in focus, very clearly shows the action being undertaken, is not cluttered with people or non essentials and is part of a logical sequence.

Selecting the right visual aid for the message

Objective
To give participants a logical basis for selecting the right visual aid for a given situation.

Organization
   Below is a list of situations and a list of possible visual aids. Make a selection of the most suitable visual aids for each situation.

Situations
   – Meeting of poor families to discuss action on malaria eradication. Meet by a canal.
   – Progressive farmers discussing the cost savings of a new tillage system. In a classroom.
   – Family planning meeting of whole village. At village hall.
   – Women's group demonstration of correct cooking of vegetables. Group leader's house.
   – Bean planting demonstration for farmers. In a garden.
   – Large public meeting to discuss how to prevent forest fires. In school hall.
   – Visit to farmer to discuss new dairy enterprise. At farm.
   – School talk about insects and crop damage. Classroom and garden.

Possible visual aids
   Slides, actual materials, loudspeakers, leaflets, poster, wall chart, taped message, flash cards, puppets, blackboard, flannelgraph, flip chart, model, samples, newsprint pad, drama group.

Discussion
   Have one or two participants lead a discussion on the choices made.

The Ambition Game

Objective
   For participants to try to determine what are their main personal motivations, and how such motivations may affect attitudes to innovations.

Method
   (a) Each participant writes down three of his ambitions.
   (b) Make a grid on the blackboard filling in each person's ambitions.
   (c) Try to put similar ambitions together.
   (d) Add up the scores (see Example overleaf).

Example grid

Participants	Ambitions						Total
	1	2	3	4	5	6	
A to be good at job	x		x	x			3
B to be richer	x	x	x		x	x	5
C to be beautiful				x			1
D to be promoted	x				x		2
E to be socially successful		x			x	x	3
F to be strong			x				1
G to serve the community				x		x	2
H to become learned		x					1

Note: A, E, G have 'prestige' components: they give a person social standing and importance in the community.

Discussion

Discuss the results and consider whether these ambitions may also apply in large part to farmers.

Participants may decide that the main human motivations are to have more money or goods and to receive more prestige or recognition. If this is so, then any messages or proposed innovations should appeal to those ambitions, otherwise they will not be accepted.

5 Teaching methods and skills

Certain procedures will help the work of Change Agents who are teaching in a classroom, for instance, holding a formal meeting, or helping to run a training course, or giving lessons at a local school. Most of the skills described here will also be valuable for informal teaching.

Objectives

By the end of this chapter you should be:
(a) Aware of the main requirements of successful classroom teaching.
(b) Able to formulate objectives and write lesson plans.
(c) Give a presentation which is interesting and informative.

Definitions of words used

lesson	– part of a course of teaching
lesson objective	– the learning aim of the lesson
lesson plan	– a written plan showing the order of the events in the lesson
training gap	– the difference between what a student knows and what he is required to know for his job
'elicit'	– to draw out thoughts and ideas from the participants.
'probe'	– to enquire more deeply, to ask additional questions.

Introduction: Classroom teaching

Those people who use some kind of classroom teaching in their work will realize that this method has both advantages and disadvantages, whether the classroom is in a school or a training centre, or even if it is just a few benches and a blackboard beneath a shady tree.

Advantages

(a) By comparison with demonstrations, classroom teaching is easy to organize and conduct, and fewer facilities are necessary.
(b) By comparison with individual visits, the Agent is working

with a large audience. This means that the cost per member of the audience is low, and you can be sure that everybody is getting the same information at the same time.

(c) By comparison with mass media, it is very flexible. It allows the Agent's message to be adapted easily to the audience's needs and to their level of understanding.

Disadvantages

(a) By comparison with other methods, it is easily misused. Without planning and careful presentation many other methods, such as demonstrations or mass media, cannot exist, but – because it is easy to give a lesson without preparation – it is easy to give a bad lesson.

(b) Adults may not wish to be taught in the classroom style.

(c) The result of these disadvantages is that lessons often lack relevance or interest. How often has the reader listened to a lecture where he never seemed to learn anything useful, because the lesson was badly prepared?

Teaching adults

Teaching adults is very different from teaching children. The main differences are:

(a) Adults will only learn those things that they perceive will be of use to them, and they need time to decide just what is useful. Children, on the other hand, see anything new as a challenge.

(b) Once having decided to learn something, adults are more strongly motivated than children.

(c) Adults have a wide knowledge and experience and expect to be treated as equals and not inferiors.

(d) Adults are generally more conservative than children.

(e) Adults have little time available because of other commitments.

A 'manager of learning'

Too often in teaching the teacher considers that he knows everything and that he is there to pour out his knowledge to the students. This is an authoritarian or dictatorial form of teaching which is unsatisfactory and ineffective when teaching adults.

You must make every effort to get away from this traditional approach to teaching. The teacher must see himself as a 'manager of learning', who is there to help his students learn and discover new ideas for themselves.

Main requirements for teaching

Research has shown that there are three important requirements for successful adult education:

(a) Involvement of students   (b) Purpose   (c) Feedback

Figure 24   Managing the learning process

---
1. Provide *knowledge* sources
2. Provide *information* sources
3. Arrange *practical* work
4. Increase students' *critical faculties* by encouraging students to:
    (a) listen–observe
    (b) ask questions
    (c) analyse
    (d) criticise

(a) *Involvement of students:* The learner should be 'active' in the process of learning. This can be achieved by allowing discussion, by encouraging people to ask questions, and by constantly relating your subject matter to the interests and environment of the audience.

(b) *Purpose:* Your subject matter should be problem-oriented. The audience must be told at the beginning of the lesson what the objectives of each lesson are, and they must understand why it is important to them. This will concentrate their attention.

(c) *Feedback:* The teaching methods used should encourage a response from the audience. By asking the audience questions, and inviting them to comment on the subject matter, you will be able to judge how well they understand you, and how relevant the information is. In this way you can adjust your presentation to make sure that people are learning something, and that what they are learning is useful to them.

These three requirements all involve interaction between the Change Agent and his audience. Both are working together to create a learning experience.

The remainder of this chapter deals with the planning and presentation of lessons in the classroom.

Planning

Planning a lesson involves two stages:
   (a) Establishing the objectives of a lesson.
   (b) Writing a lesson plan based on these objectives.

Carrying out both stages will help to ensure that each lesson is serving a purpose as effectively as possible. If you do not establish objectives and write plans, then you will give poor lessons.

You should start the planning process by answering the following questions about each lesson:
Who are you going to present it to?
Why are you going to present it?
What are you going to present?
How are you going to present it?

Who are you going to present it to?

You must start by defining your students. These are the people who will benefit from the lesson. Once you know exactly who they are, then you can ensure that your objective is relevant to their needs. (See Audience characteristics, Fig 11 in Chapter 2.) Draw up a description of the students, so that a course can be prepared at a suitable level for them. What, then, are their characteristics?

Physical: Age, sex, home area.
Education: Present knowledge and skills, language, vocabulary, previous learning style.
Social: Attitudes, beliefs, interests, expectations, motivations, social status, authority.
Socio-economic: Level of income, occupations.

Why are you going to present it?

You must next decide what knowledge or skills your audience should have at the end of each lesson. What do you aim to achieve?

The answer to this question is your main objective. It enables you to evaluate the relevance of the subject matter and the effectiveness of the presentation. Because of this link with evaluation, the objective should be clearly stated in measurable terms. A statement like 'At the end of the lesson the audience should know about making compost' is not a good objective. This is because it does not say how you can measure whether or not it has been achieved. A better objective would be 'At the end of the lesson the audience should be able to describe accurately the six steps to making good compost'. You can measure how well this objective has been achieved by asking members of the audience to describe how compost is made. In this way you can decide if a further or better explanation is needed.

An objective, therefore, needs an aim (i.e. what is to be achieved) and a measurable element (i.e. to what level, or in what way the aim should be achieved).

What are you going to present?

You must now select your subject matter according to what you want the audience to understand. You must decide precisely what technical information they need to know, what this represents in practical terms, how this differs from their present practices, and the reason why they should change their practices.

The Change Agent's purpose in selecting subject matter is to close the gap between the present level of knowledge which his audience has and the level of knowledge which is needed to fulfil the objective. Subject matter which is not helping close this gap is not only unnecessary, it may also be confusing. The ability to select appropriate subject matter is an important skill which every Change Agent should develop.

Figure 25 The training gap

	Knowledge and skills necessary for the job
minus	Existing knowledge and skills
equals	Training required

For the purpose of planning interesting and informative lessons it is also important to consider the order in which the subject matter will be presented.

This order is not always easy to decide upon, but here are a few guidelines which will be useful:

(a) Start by telling the audience what the objectives of the lesson are and why the subject is important. In this way they will immediately know the relevance of the lesson and they will listen more carefully.

(b) Make sure that the link between one piece of information and another is clearly understood.

(c) If you are describing a process, then describe the events that make up that process in the order in which they occur.

(d) Make your presentation interesting by spreading out the use of teaching aids (blackboard, overhead transparencies, slides, etc.). For example, rather than talking for 30 minutes and then showing six pictures all at once, show pictures at well-spaced intervals.

(e) Also, give examples and ask questions at regular intervals.

(f) Always finish by repeating the most important points. Repetition in teaching is important.

How are you going to present it?

You must finally decide what teaching methods and aids you will use. Should you give a lecture or hold a discussion? Should you use a blackboard or show a film strip? These are the kinds of questions that must be answered.

Other chapters in this book will help you answer some of these questions. For example, Chapter 4 deals with the selection of appropriate media, and Chapter 2 discusses the analysis of target audiences.

Now you can write your lesson plan. The plan should also include instructions to yourself. These will tell you when to use training aids, as well as remind you when to ask questions. There must be sufficient time allowed for demonstrations, discussion, practice and repetition.

Visits to places of interest which are relevant to the lesson are an important activity. Often, however, students are taken long distances, wasting much time, in order to see a 'super farmer'. It is much better to select a farmer close by. The fact that the farming operation may have a number of faults may be a useful part of the lesson.

Example of a lesson plan

(a) Preparing for the lesson

Title

Lesson content

Objective
(measurable increase in student knowledge, skill or attitude)

Suggested location

Seating arrangements

Equipment and materials required*

Visual aid equipment required*

Visual aids required*

* Assemble and check before lesson.

(b) The lesson

1. **Introduction**
   Tell class the content of the lesson and desired result.

2. **Lead in from previous training**
   Explained by teacher.

3. **Student experience**
   Elicited by teacher.

4. **Core lecture**
   Main points. May need several sheets of paper.

5. **Student activity**
   Select and organize.
   Visit.

6. **Discussion or report**
   Organized by teacher on points arising from activities.

7. **Round up**
   Summary of main points by teacher.

8. **Next related lesson**
   Briefly outlined by teacher.

Time in classroom _____ hours   Lesson prepared by _____

Time on outside activity ____ hours   Checked/Approved by _____

Presentation

Many people, when they have to speak to a large group, get nervous, or the group does not seem to be interested. Here are some suggestions which should help you to speak easily and effectively. Most of these suggestions are just common sense, or are the natural outcome of the planning process just described. However, they are worth repeating because you should have no problem in being a good teacher, if you can put these simple things into practice.

Avoiding nervousness

Most people are nervous when they start teaching. These points will help you.

(a) Plan your lesson in advance.

(b) Rehearse what you have to say, using the visual aids you plan to use.

(c) When giving the presentation do not try to memorize everything. Use your lesson plan to remind you of the subject matter, or have notes written on small cards which you can keep in your hand.

Keeping your audience interested

This is essential if a lesson is to be effective. It is also easy to do if you plan your lesson in the way which has been described above.

(a) Make sure you have something specific and relevant to say, and be enthusiastic about it.

(b) Ask your audience questions, and encourage them to ask you questions.

(c) Give plenty of examples.

(d) Use plenty of visual aids. However, do not spend a lot of time drawing on a blackboard or setting up a projector, etc. Prepare these things in advance.

(e) Arrange the seating so that it suits the purpose of the lesson. (See diagram of possible seating arrangements.)

(f) Do not forget to stop the lesson or change the activity when people seem to get bored. There is no point in teaching if people have lost their concentration.

Helping your audience to understand

Some of what you have to tell people will be new to them, so it is important not to hurry when you teach. Take it slowly.

(a) Use words and phrases that people will understand.

(b) Test your visual aids on friends to make sure that they are easily understood.

(c) Do not try to present too much information at once. It is better to present two of three lessons which people understand rather than one which confuses your audience.

(d) Do not forget to ask questions to find out if people do understand.

Helping your audience to remember

Your audience is there to learn something. To learn something effectively they must not only understand it, but also remember it. You can make it easier by:

(a) Being as clear as possible. Information in addition to what is essential will act as a distraction. People have a relatively short concentration span so this should not be wasted on inessential information.

(b) Reinforce your main points with the use of visual aids. People learn best through their eyes.
(c) Always repeat the main points at the end. If you only hear something once, you usually do not remember it.
(d) Whenever possible, distribute printed material which summarizes your lesson.
(e) And do not forget to 'follow up' your lesson. Visit people to remind them of the information and repeat your message at other meetings.

Avoiding distractions

If there is something else going on which people can focus their attention on, they will. There are a number of common distractions which you should take care to avoid:
(a) Hand out printed material at the end of the lesson, otherwise people will be looking at it while you are talking.
(b) Hold the meeting in a room where people are not going to be walking in and out.
(c) If people start talking you can regain their attention by raising your voice a little, moving about, asking a question, or starting to use a visual aid.

Finally, be considerate

It is always important to give proper respect to your audience.
(a) Do not talk to your audience as if they are children.
(b) Ask their opinions and find out their problems.
(c) Make sure everybody can see and hear.
(d) Dress appropriately.
(e) Do not forget to thank those who have helped to arrange the lesson.

Self-study exercises

1. One of the best ways to study what makes a good lesson – or a bad one – is actually to watch lessons being presented. Visit a local school or training centre, or watch a colleague holding a meeting. Judge what you see according to what you have learnt in the lesson.
You might find it useful to draw up an evaluation form before you start and use it as a checklist of questions to ask yourself. An example is shown on page 79.
2. A good way of practising teaching skills is by micro-teaching. This is where a very short lesson is given for training purposes.
You can do this with a small group of colleagues. Each person prepares a 'lesson' of 5–10 minutes and presents it to the others. You can then discuss what you think are the good and bad points of each other's presentation. Remember, however, that a teacher needs confidence, and any counselling should help build this up.
3. Why should an objective be stated in measurable terms?

Figure 26   Possible seating arrangements

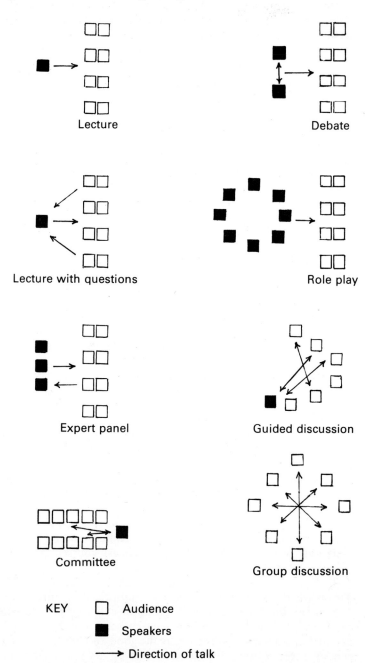

Guide for supervision of teaching.

There are certain skills/activities which a teacher can use to improve his/her teaching. A supervisor can attend a session and subsequently advise and help the teacher improve his/her weak points.

Comments

1. Did the teacher introduce himself/herself?
2. Did the teacher introduce the subject and objective of lesson?
3. Was there a link with the previous lesson or experience?
4. Was student experience elicited?
5. Did the teacher elicit and probe with questions?
6. Were there activities for the participants?
7. Was the teacher responsive and warm? Did he use praise?
8. How did the teacher react to interruption, inattention, lateness, rudeness?
9. How did the teacher cope with difficult questions?
10. Did the teacher use personal movement to create more interest?
11. Did he wear appropriate dress and avoid distracting personal habits?
12. Did he use appropriate language and speak clearly?
13. Did he use visuals and examples to illustrate points?
14. Did he write clearly on the blackboard?
15. Does he know his subject?
16. Did he repeat and reinforce important points?
17. Did he sum up well at the end of the lesson?
18. Was the lesson planned beforehand?
19. Were the visuals prepared beforehand?
20. Were the seating and organizing arrangements satisfactory?

6 Managing training courses

This chapter will be of particular interest for those people involved with managing courses. It is concerned with the need for courses and how to organize and manage them.

Objectives

By the end of this chapter you should be able to:
(a) List the main problems in course management.
(b) Evaluate a course through student evaluation.
(c) Know the main problems in course management.

Introduction: Is a course really necessary?

Change Agents will sometimes be involved in running training courses. These may be one day courses for small groups or more complex courses at a training centre. Each Change Agent therefore needs to know the methods used in running courses.

The very first point, though, is to determine whether or not a training course is really necessary. Too often when there is a problem

---

Figure 27   Optimum length of courses

Minimum course length

Course components: creation of interest
theoretical knowledge
technical information
demonstrations and visits
practice and confidence building
tests and evaluation

Useful additional time

Repetition and reinforcement

Unnecessary time on course

Leads to: worry about home and family
boring course
overcrowded training facilities
greatly increased costs
own job neglected

of low production, or failure to take up an innovation, the assumption is made that training will resolve the situation. But it may be, for example, that the product price is too low, or that the innovation is technically unsuitable. (Training courses cannot of themselves solve such problems.) If, however, it can be established that training is essential to teach a new skill, help change an attitude, or improve co-operation between farmers, then courses should be undertaken.

In other words, there must be a very clear purpose or objective for holding a course.

Pre-course planning

Some personal details about the students can be obtained before the course, which will help in planning the lessons and their content. Each student can be sent a questionnaire to complete and return (see the example questionnaire).

Example of a questionnaire for course participant

Name .... Age .... Sex ....

Home Address ....

Job Title ....

Work Place ....

What do you specialize in? ....
....

What training have you had? ....
....

How much field experience do you have? ....

Years/Months ....

How long have you been on the present job? ....

Years/Months ....

Have you ever attended any in-service courses on communication? (If so, specify) ....
....
....

For what reasons are you attending the course here? ....
....
....

When will you arrive for the course?

Date .... Time ....

Figure 28   Essentials for training courses

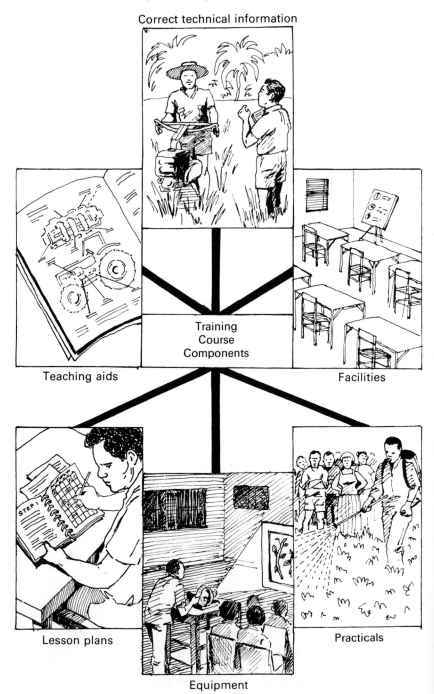

Arrangements before the participants arrive

Do you run your courses like a hotel manager or like a prison officer? Most people say 'hotel manager', which means you must think of every eventuality so that your guests want to return. A course is only succesful if participants want to return for a follow-up course.

One wrong thing, such as bad food, can easily cause trouble to such an extent that participants will resent the whole course no matter how good the content is. There are many factors that need to be considered.

Evaluation of training course arrangements

Accommodation
Is it adequate? Enough rooms, enough beds?
Have you checked the:
    Cleaning arrangements?
    Laundry facilities?
    Mosquito nets, spray?
    Security?
    Bedding?
    Ventilation?

Food
Will there be enough?
Are the mealtimes arranged?
Is the dining hall ready?

Entertainment
What have you arranged?
What facilities are there, e.g., games, table-tennis, football?
Is there a radio/TV?
Can newspapers be delivered?

Transport
Is there a suitable bus to the town centre?
If not, can transport be arranged?

Information
Have you a list of the facilities available both at the training centre and locally (e.g., bus numbers and timing; churches, shops, mealtimes; sporting facilities)?
Does each room have details of what to do in an emergency and where staff can be contacted at night?

Lecture facilities
Are they comfortable, clean, tidy?
Does the projection equipment work?
Has the projectionist been informed as to when he is required?
Is there sufficient chalk and a duster?
Have lecturers been reminded of the timetable?

If you are in charge of a course or training centre, complete the evaluation list and see how you rate. If you have just attended a course, then rate the arrangements.

Timetables

A well designed timetable is the key to a well-organized course, but it requires thought. Some points to bear in mind:

(a) Check when lecturers are available *before* writing the timetable, not afterwards.

(b) Where possible put the academically 'heavier' sessions in the morning and 'lighter' practical-based sessions in the afternoon.

(c) Slot films into the timetable to break lectures up and refresh tired participants.

(d) Allow time for participants to sort out any non-course business. It is far better for the whole group to miss a day than to have odd people wandering in and out all week.

(e) The first day should be reasonably relaxed, but still relevant to the objectives of the course.

(f) It is a mistake to cram too much into the evenings and far better to allow participants to relax and talk informally. However, if evenings are to be used, then films and light discussion are recommended.

(g) Flexibility is important, as lecturers may not keep to time. Flexibility can be achieved by:
1. Having sessions of standard length, e.g., 30 minutes, 1 hour, $1\frac{1}{2}$ hours, etc., so that switching can be done.
2. Having a film on 'stand-by'.
3. Having an exercise or some individual work that participants can do.
4. Identifying lecturers who are available at very short notice.

Course co-ordinator

A course co-ordinator should be selected to ensure the smooth running of a course. The co-ordinator has a vital role to play. He must:

– Create a link between each session as well as introducing each day.

– Introduce lecturers and participants. (A good way to introduce participants to each other is to give everyone five minutes to chat to his neighbour, then to have each person introduce his neighbour. This produces much better introductions and initial participation than if each person merely introduces himself.)

– Ensure that the seating and classroom arrangements are satisfactory.

– Ensure that lecturers attend their sessions and keep to time.

– Check and arrange that necessary audio-visual equipment is available and working.

Introductory session

Students' expectations

Participants starting a course will have widely different expectations and anxieties which may include:
- Not being sure what the course objectives are.
- Resentment at being away from home or the office.
- Regarding the course as a holiday at government expense.
- High expectations that the course will teach a lot and prove useful.
- Participants not knowing each other and being afraid to express themselves.

To overcome these problems, a well-organized first session is necessary, with a discussion on the course objectives. This is also a good time for everyone to be introduced.

Student participation

Trainees must be made to feel involved and to have a considerable say in the way the course is to be run. It is a good idea to let participants have a representative through whom they can channel their problems. Allow a certain flexibility in the timetable for participants to add or subtract sessions which they wish changed.

Audio-visual materials for courses

Trainers need to make plans well in advance so that they can have useful audio-visual materials for the courses.

Films

Training films provide useful resource material for a course. Films are expensive to buy, but can usually be borrowed cheaply either locally or from one of the international libraries.

Possible local sources of films

Embassies and cultural centres, e.g., British Council, French Cultural Centre, oil companies, airlines, ministries, training colleges, broadcasting stations, UN offices.

International libraries

These libraries often have an office in the main towns and can arrange for films to be sent free of charge. It can take 3–4 weeks to obtain a film, so order well in advance.
FAO Film Loan Library, Information Division
Via delle Termedi Caracalle
00100 Rome
Italy

(FAO has a large library including a number of films devoted to rural development and extension training.)

US Agency for International Development
Bureau of Population and Humanitarian Assistance
Washington D.C.20523
USA

UNICEF
United Nations
New York
NY 10017
USA

World Health Organization
Palais des Nations
CH 1211 Geneva
Switzerland

United Agency for International Development (USAID)
Washington D.C. 20523
USA

World Bank
1818 H. Street N.W.
Washington D.C. 20433
USA

UNESCO
Press and Audiovisual Information Division
Office of Public Information
Place de Fontenoy
75007 Paris
France

Film viewing reports

It is useful to keep a critical report of each film viewed for future reference. This could be broken into areas, i.e., management, teaching extension methods, rural development, visual aids, communication theory, entertainment. The report should include where the film can be borrowed, its reference number, its length, when made, and whether colour or black and white. When making comments, assess the audience it is suitable for and give a brief outline of the film and the sessions it can be used in. Do not hesitate to state if a film is unsuitable so that your colleagues do not have the embarrassment of showing an unsuitable film to an audience.

Slides, posters, wall charts

Ministry resource centres should be able to help provide these. The training centre should be equipped with a camera so that slide sets on subject matter and local interest pictures can be produced. Commercial firms are often very willing to supply excellent wall charts on technical subjects such as machinery, plant protection, animal health, etc.

Flannelgraphs, models, puppets
These can be manufactured by the training centre itself or supplied by the organization's resource centre.

Back-up papers, handouts
Again, these can be produced by the centre or organization and may be offset printed or stencilled.

Training records and evaluation

You should get participants to evaluate the course. Student evaluation may be verbal or written. Verbal evaluation can lead to a consensus between participants with conflicting views. Written evaluation allows individuals to make pointed criticisms without identification as long as the questionnaire is anonymous! A combination of evaluation methods often brings the most useful feedback.

Verbal evaluation
Try to encourage the whole group to discuss the points so that some kind of group opinion can be noted. Tackle both the course content as well as non-course facilities such as food, accommodation and entertainment.

Written evaluation
A questionnaire is the easiest way of obtaining a written response. An example is given below, but this may need to vary from course to course.

Example of a training evaluation form

To help the organizers of the training programme improve their course, please rate the training you have received by drawing a circle around the appropriate number.

	Good	Fair	Poor
1. Value of this training in relation to my job.	3	2	1
2. The usefulness of the subject matter content.	3	2	1
3. The presentation methods used.	3	2	1
4. Trainer's ability to transfer knowledge.	3	2	1
5. Participants encouraged to participate.	3	2	1
6. My opinions were listened to.	3	2	1

7. Value of the handouts.	3	2	1
8. Use of audio-visual instructional media.	3	2	1
9. Duration of this training	Too long	Appropriate	Too short

10. Did this training attain its objectives?

   ....

   ....

11. What did you *like* most about this training?

   ....

   ....

Training records

A trainer should keep records of courses and students. This should include an assessment of their performance, which will help in selecting students for advanced courses.

Example of a training record

Name..................... Address ....

....

Date entered service ....

Designation ....

Expertise ....

Course			
Dates	Title	Grade A, B or C	Comments

Planning and reporting

The manager of a training centre will have to submit work plans and reports each year. The best way to do this is to consider each activity in turn.

Example of a planning and reporting guide for training centres

1. List available resources – building, equipment, etc.
2. Available funds and budget – sources, amounts.
3. Consider teaching activities – timetable, lesson plans, teaching aids, practical work.
4. Conducting exams – how, where, when.
5. Sports, cultural activities entertainment – indoor, games, outdoor games, drama, clubs, religious affairs.
6. Library – books, magazines.
7. Management of campus – gardens, roads.
8. Management of hostel – kitchen, bathrooms, toilets, student rooms, bedrooms
9. Maintenance of buildings
10. Farm – cropping scheme, inputs, labour.
11. Maintenance of workshop
12. Office management
13. Transport
14. Utilities – electricity, water supply.
15. Security

Self-study guide

1. When is it necessary to run a training course and when might this be waste of time?
2. What will cause students to become dissatisfied with the course management?
3. Why might you need a course co-ordinator? What is his role?
4. What is the purpose of having the students evaluate a course?

7 Supervising staff

In your career you may be expected at some stage to supervise the work of other Change Agents. Thus some information on the management of people is included here. It covers the attitudes which employees may have, the management role and responsibilities, and staff discipline, development and counselling. Finally, the management of your time is discussed.

Objectives

By the end of this chapter you should be able to:
 (a) Define the role of a supervisor.
 (b) Explain the need to delegate work and responsibilities.
 (c) Explain how time is wasted and what steps can be taken to prevent this.

Definitions of words used

agenda – items to be considered at a meeting
authority – power, right to act
counselling – talking over what is to be done, advising
delegate – to give authority to a person to act
ego – self, self-conceit
illusion – deceptive appearance
responsible – accountable, answerable
rubber stamp – agreement without examination
supervise – to oversee, direct work
subordinate – person working under another

Introduction: A manager's job

An individual has to organize his own activities. He has to be careful in deciding objectives and priorities; he has to plan out his work bearing in mind how much time is available.

With a number of people under him this becomes even more complex. The work of all these people has to be co-ordinated. In addition, the human problems that arise have to be dealt with in the least disruptive way.

The managers two main responsibilities are:
 (a) To carry out the wishes and instructions of his organization.

This is, after all, what he is paid to do. He is not being paid to follow his own plans and own ambitions.

(b) To look after his subordinates – their welfare, working conditions and morale. If he fails to do this, then he is unlikely to be successful with his first responsibility.

Management styles

Supervisors behave in different ways from each other, but they may need to change their behaviour if different circumstances arise. For example, the supervisor who normally is prepared to discuss activities may, in an emergency, become dictatorial. However, most of the time each supervisor has a particular style of management.

Consider the different management styles listed below and see if they remind you of yourself or of anyone you know.

Management by Objectives (M.B.O.)
This manager has carefully planned his work based on reasoned objectives. First, he has clearly laid out the policy required by the organization. Then he and his subordinates list and agree objectives for a future period (usually one year). The subordinates carry out the objectives with the manager guiding. At the end of the period the subordinates can be evaluated by the manager and can evaluate themselves by seeing whether the objectives have been attained.

Management by Discussion (M.B.D.)
This manager likes to discuss objectives and activities with his team and obtain their views. He then makes a decision. He is generally a good manager.

Management by Mushroom (M.B.M.)
This manager treats his employees like mushrooms. He keeps them in the dark and never informs them about anything. He is frightened of his employees and doubts his own competence.

Management by Illusion (M.B.I.)
This manager is tricky; no one quite knows what his real aims are. He may say something and mean something else. Usually he is only concerned for his own advancement.

Management by Consensus (M.B.C)
This manager is afraid to make a decision. The result is endless meetings to try to obtain a group consensus decision. He is frightened of losing his job and wishes to share management risks with his staff.

Management by Bulldozer (M.B.B.)
This manager is a dictator. He runs his organization like an army, with no questions allowed. He often achieves good results, but there is no staff development and little long term future for the organization because the good staff leave.

Management by Ego (M.B.E.)
This manager is very conceited and wants to be constantly flattered. Those who do not flatter him are discharged.

Activities of supervisors

The supervisor has a wide range of responsibilities and some of the most important ones are listed below. The priority which each responsibility takes will vary from programme to programme and will also depend on the job description which has been given to the supervisor by his or her organization. Study each responsibility listed below and work out what this would involve in your own situation. Choose the five you think most important.
- (a) Improve work methods used by staff.
- (b) Handle complaints.
- (c) Develop subordinates' skill.
- (d) Set goals and objectives.
- (e) Make firm decisions.
- (f) Set high standards in your own work.
- (g) Encourage and praise good work.
- (h) Build teamwork and harmony between staff.
- (i) Direct and control staff activities.
- (j) Encourage group decisions.
- (k) Ensure good staff discipline.
- (l) Regular check of subordinates' programmes.
- (m) Sack poor staff.
- (n) Organize staff training.
- (o) Delegate work.

Attitudes of employees

Many traditional supervisors believe that employees are naturally lazy and need to be driven. Other supervisors do not think this is true, believing that employees possess valuable potential and will do well, given skilful management and encouragement.

Consider the points in the two lists below and decide which you think is true.

List (a) Traditional
1. People are naturally lazy; they prefer to do nothing.
2. People work mostly for money and status rewards.
3. The main force keeping people productive is their fear of being demoted or fired.
4. People expect and depend on direction from above; they do not want to think for themselves.
5. People need to be told, shown and trained in proper methods of work.

List (b) Potential
1. People seek many satisfactions in work: pride in achievement,

sense of contribution, pleasure in association, stimulation of new challenges.

2. The main force keeping people productive in their work is desire to achieve their personal and social goals.

3. People close to the situation see and feel what is needed and are capable of self-direction.

4. People need to sense that they are respected as capable of assuming responsibility.

5. People seek self-realization; jobs must be designed, modified and fitted to people.

It is now generally thought that what employees are really looking for is recognition that they are doing a good job. This is their most important requirement. After that – of course – the employee wants more money, good housing, better working conditions, etc.

Thus the supervisor needs to give encouragement and praise for good work and initiative. The employee must feel that the organization and his supervisor supports and encourages him, and that good work will be rewarded.

Counselling

The supervisor must develop skills of counselling his employees and be able to advise them about their work and living problems. If they are not working well, he must try to find out the problem and help to solve it. This requires tact and kindness.

Discipline

Every now and again a person on the staff is useless or damaging to the organization and no amount of counselling will change this. The supervisor must be prepared to remove this person from the staff, however unpleasant a task this may be. What the supervisor must not do is to allow the difficulties to become personal between himself and the employee. Any termination notices should be written by a person higher up in the organization.

Delegation

Many supervisors are overworked. This is because they have not learnt to delegate work to the employees. They perhaps consider that the employees are too inexperienced, or they are afraid of giving an employee a chance to show how good he is.

Some supervisors may give the 'responsibility' of a task to an employee, but fail to pass on the necessary 'authority' for the employee adequately to undertake the task. The rule is that you must 'give authority when you give responsibility'.

A manager should spend much of his time planning, thinking, problem solving and checking on new activities. Routine work should be delegated.

Staff development
Managers should encourage their staff to develop their skills and knowledge. Training and opportunities for self-study and correspondence courses should be organized. The supervisor can sometimes obtain technical books and magazines, and arrange for visits to places of interest.

Job descriptions
A supervisor will ensure that each of his staff has a clear job description so that there is no confusion about their roles and responsibilities. Periodically, he should discuss with each member of staff how he is getting on in relation to his job description.

Meetings
Some supervisors enjoy meetings. Many people do. They are cosy warm activities. Nobody has to do much work; any decisions made are collective decisions and therefore there is no risk of any one person being blamed for making the wrong decisions. Meetings should not be an excuse for 'collective irresponsibility'.

However, meetings are necessary. In particular, a weekly or fortnightly meeting promotes a good group feeling, and people can air their problems before they grow too big. Meetings must be controlled and kept short, otherwise people become bored and time is wasted.

Basically, there are four sorts of meetings:

(a) *Information meeting*

To inform staff of events or activities. These are important meetings, but should be kept brief. Staff should not be informed of events which are only possibilities. This will merely upset them and work will suffer. Only inform them of events which will definitely happen.

(b) *Discussion meeting*

To discuss or plan some action. All such meetings should have an agenda which should be circulated well before the meeting, so that individuals can think carefully about the subject for discussion.

The agenda should state the subject for discussion and also what exactly has to be decided. It there are a number of items on the agenda, then a time limit for discussion can be written against each item. Obviously the more important items will be given the most time.

(c) *Rubber stamp meeting*

A meeting called by the supervisor to attempt to obtain agreement by the staff to his views on a particular subject. Such meetings are a waste of time. The supervisor should make the decision himself and face up to his responsibilities.

(d) *Open chat meeting*

A rambling free-for-all discussion. Try to be absent from it. Nothing will be resolved.

Management of time

Time is the only currency of an Extension service and it must not be wasted. How often do you come to the end of the day wondering where the time has gone and how much you have achieved? Below is a list of time wasters. Which ones are you guilty of? Do you agree with the suggested solutions?

Time waster	Possible causes	Solutions
Muddled, confused work.	Failure to see the benefit of planning.	Recognize that planning takes time, but saves time in the end.
	Lack of goals and objectives.	Write down goals and objectives. Discuss priorities with subordinates.
Overcommitment	Too broad interests.	Say 'no' to extra requests.
	Failure to set priorities.	Put first things first.
Visitors	Enjoyment of socializing.	Do it elsewhere. Meet visitors outside.
	Inability to say no (unstructured meetings).	Try to say 'no'. Be unavailable. Be busy.
Telephone	Lack of self-discipline.	Be brief. When calling make a note of the points before dialling.
Meetings	Fear of responsibility for decisions.	Make decisions without holding meetings.
	Too much information.	Discourage unnecessary meetings.
	Poor leadership.	Use agenda. Stick to the subject. Prepare concise minutes as soon as possible.
Lack of delegation.	Fear of subordinates' inadequacy.	Train. Allow mistakes.
	Fear of subordinates' competence.	Delegate fully. Give credit.

Figure 29 Management of time – but not like this!

Self-study questions

1. What is counselling of staff?
2. What is the role of a supervisor?
3. Why are some supervisors afraid to delegate work?
4. What are the main time wasters?
5. Explain what is an agenda for a meeting?

Group activity studies

Boss Game

To be played by a small group of Agents at a training course.

Objective

To give participants at a course an appreciation of what really makes a good boss or supervisor or manager. To give participants some idea of their own ability as a manager or organizer.

Method

List the characteristics which participants think make a good boss (see the example for extra ideas). Then participants write down an alias name for bosses they have worked under or have known. They score each characteristic for each boss out of a maximum of 4. Add up the total marks for each boss.

Discussion

Are there any common factors for good bosses or bad bosses? If all your bosses have well over half marks, your critical faculty needs sharpening. If you have mostly given them low marks, are you perhaps too critical and dissatisfied?

Score how you see yourself. How do you rate? If you are not a supervisor, how do you think you would rate?

Example of characteristics for the Boss Game

Good characteristics of supervisor	e.g. Joe Brown	Alias of person you have worked under or know					Yourself
Clear objectives	2						
Good planner	2						

Good organizer	1						
Gets staff to participate in decisions	1						
Keeps staff informed	2						
Truthful	4						
Good meeting chairman	3						
Considerate to staff	4						
Sense of humour	3						
Total	22						

Supervisor's Game

Objective
    For participants to understand that there are different types of management; realizing this early on will help the supervisor recognize his own faults.

Method
    Participants, in pairs, act out the different roles which a supervisor may take. One person should be the supervisor, the other an employee.
    The organizer secretly informs each pair what management type they should portray. Each pair has five minutes to prepare a three minute role play.
    After the role play, the other participants will attempt to describe the type of manager which each pair has portrayed.

    Suggestions for management types
        Management by Objectives (M.B.O.) – work and objective orientated.
        Management by Mushroom (M.B.M.) – keeping employees in the dark.
        Management by Shouting (M.B.S.) – everyone shouts.

Management by Illusion (M.B.I.) — a devious manager who is untruthful.

Management by Politics (M.B.P.) — concentrating on survival, his personal safety; does not like strong subordinates; plays at office politics.

Management by Reason (M.B.R.) — listening to and working with subordinates; clear logical decisions.

Management by Bulldozer (M.B.B.) — uninterested in anyone else's ideas.

8 Planning and evaluating programmes

How planning should be undertaken and methods of collecting data are discussed in this chapter.

Objectives

By the end of the chapter you should be able to:
(a) Explain the need to collect basic data.
(b) Write clear objectives.
(c) List the items which should be considered when writing a work plan.
(d) Explain the reasons for undertaking evaluation.

Definitions of words used

aim	– to give direction to, direct effort towards
evaluate	– to judge, to count numerically
implement	– to undertake an activity
needs assessment	– a study of a community to determine what the community itself wants and requires
objective	– something aimed at, direction of action
programme plan	– a long range plan, usually detailed
side effect	– the unplanned reaction to an activity
survey	– to measure, examine
technical innovation	– a scientific or mechanical new method
work plan	– a detailed plan of what to do, how and when to do it.

Introduction: National aims

Governments normally have long range plans for the development of the country. This chapter is concerned with plans for rural areas. They are usually designed to help improve the welfare of those in the rural area, and also to raise production and keep food prices down. Any development organization has to take these aims into account in its own planning, and attempt to fulfil the wishes of the government. However, these aims are usually broad, and it is up to the planners to design meaningful programmes within these aims.

Figure 30   Rural development plan

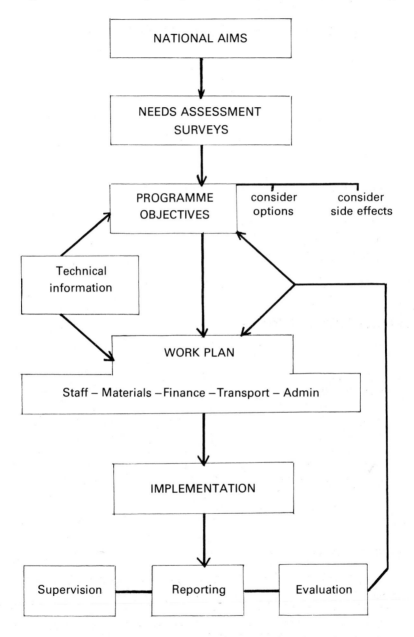

Needs assessment

Before making any decisions about development strategies it is obviously necessary to study the community so that you can determine the needs and ambitions of the people. This is a 'needs assessment study'.

The needs assessment involves working with the community or group and, through discussion and examination, finding out what the community is interested in doing and what it considers it needs. If certain of these needs are outside the scope of the organization, then the relevant organization should be informed. The needs that are within the organization's scope should, if possible, be dealt with in the priority order determined by the community. Thus, if the community wants help with introducing mango trees rather than a programme aimed at planting more rice, then mangoes should be the priority. The rice can come later. Only in this way will the community feel that the Change Agent is on their side.

Resources of the area

Before you can start on any specific development you need to know a great deal about the people. This is called 'human resources'. Your area also contains natural and infrastructural resources, which you must find out about. We need to know:
   (a) The people's knowledge, education, local government and leadership.
   (b) The activities and roles of the women.
   (c) The health of people and medical resources.
   (d) Their skills and farming practices.
   (e) The natural resources of the area and climatic data.
   (f) The infrastructural resources, e.g., roads, electricity, markets.
   (g) Production of crops, marketing and storage systems.
   (h) Schools and training facilities, etc.

Much of this information may be available in reports, in files or in the memories of staff. Other information will have to be collected by survey.

The survey

Information is usually needed quickly and should not cost a lot to collect. Probably a 5 per cent or even smaller sample will suffice.

When undertaking the survey a careful explanation of the purpose and friendliness towards farmers are necessary. Questions must be carefully and politely phrased. Some people feel that education gives them a natural right to act in a superior way to those who have no or little education. Education to them means what is learnt in school or at training colleges. So in a village they feel they are in authority.

A farmer may have little formal education, but he will have acquired a lot of knowledge from various sources throughout his life; he may know more about certain practical farming activities than the

Change Agent. Therefore, when you get information from rural people, you have to let them know that you respect them, that you are genuinely interested in their views.

You may cause offence by asking certain questions, because different cultures find different things offensive. This can apply even to an apparently innocent question about the number of children or cattle a person has or his age or income.

It is sometimes difficult to get a farmer to state an opinion. One way round this is to ask him about what his friends or neighbours think rather than he himself. Research has shown that most people will attribute to others their own opinions when questioned in this way.

Sometimes it is better not to record or note down people's responses in front of them, as it may make them less frank. This is often the case with traditional societies. Rely on your memory and write it down as soon after the interview as you can.

Information from a carefully selected number of farmers will give the detailed data required. Below is an example of a Report Form for an individual farmer. You should, however, design a survey to suit your own specific requirements, and you may find that you do not need one as complicated as the one shown.

Example of a report form

Name of village .... Area ....

A. *Farm operator*

1. Name ....

2. Approx. age ....

3. Able to read ....

4. Members of what local organizations ....

5. Special skills (carpentry, blacksmith, weaver, etc.) ....

6. Operating this farm for .... years.

7. Religion ....

B. *Family members*

Relationship to farm operator	Age (approx)	Able to read
Wife (husband) Sons Daughters		

C. *Farm home*

Type of construction ....

Water supply (source) ....

Electricity (source) ....

Fuel used (source) ....

Kitchen garden (size, kind of vegetables) ....

D. *Farm crops (including woodlots)*

Kind	Hectares

Land tenure:

self owned .... hectares

communal .... hectares

rented .... hectares

E. *Poultry and livestock*

	Number
Cattle Goats Chickens Other	

F. *Fish*

Amount of catch last year ....

H. *Farm equipment*

Name of item
1.

    2.
    3.
    4.

L. Gross income:
1. From farm crops ....
2. From poultry and livestock ....
3. Farm fish catch ....
4. From hiring out as labour ....
5. From other wage earners in the family ....
6. Other sources ....

J. Estimate of working capital available to the farmer ....

K. Credit
Credit needed ....

L. Conditions of crops (disease, etc.)
....
....

M. Condition of livestock
....
....
1. Do the livestock appear healthy or not ....
2. What diseases are prevalent ....
3. Does the farmer supply supplementary foods in any form ......

N. Marketing
1. To whom does the farmer sell his produce ....
2. Does he obtain a loan in advance on the crops ....
3. Does the farmer market through any cooperative ....

O. Where is the nearest market and shopping centre ....

P. Diet

How frequently do they eat the following foods?
State the number of times.

	Weekly
Meat, poultry, fish	
Eggs	
Milk, fresh or tinned	
Beans, peas and groundnuts	
Vegetables	

Q. Health

Diseases suffered ....

Health facilities ....

Latrine at house ....

R. Water

Are domestic supplies adequate? ....

Where are they obtained? ....

Distance in wet season ....

Distance in dry season ....

S. Information/advice

How often are they visited by:

    Film units ....

    Change Agents ....
    (specify health, agriculture, family planning, etc.)

How often do they:

    Listen to radio ....

    Attend meetings ....

    Attend demonstrations ....

    Attend club meetings ....

Analysis of data

You will have sufficient data to make some reasoned plans. From your farmers survey, you will know their present skills and practices, and from the needs assessment you will know the ambitions of the community. Your agricultural records, surveys and experiments should give you a good idea of the potential of the area.

Programme objectives

Once all the data have been collected and analysed, programme objectives can be drawn up. These should be decided in conjunction with local leaders and farmers, as discussed in Chapter 2.

The objectives should be written in the form of clear aims with targets to achieve. Without targets it is impossible to calculate farm input requirements or to undertake planning of marketing facilities.

Here is an example of a well thought out objective:
'To increase cotton production from 500 tons to 750 tons by increasing the area being sprayed by farmers from 150 hectares to 200 hectares.'
From this objective you can calculate how much more spray and machines will be required, how many more extension staff will be needed, the extra transport and marketing, etc.

When planning objectives it is a good idea to consider what the various options are, rather than considering just one. The side effects of undertaking each option should also be considered. Some options may create good side effects, e.g., an increased demand for local labour; other options may have harmful side effects, e.g., continuous growing of cassava on poor land causing irreversible damage to the land.

Figure 31   Determining programme objectives

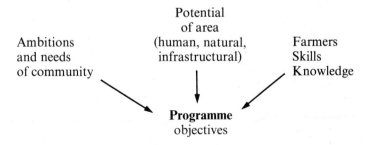

The plan should be written down. A possible format is shown below.

EXTENSION PROGRAMME PLAN

1. Geographic area
2. People concerned
3. General aim of programme
4. Objectives
   (a) Improve knowledge/understanding
   (b) Adopt new practices
   (c) Improve performance/skills
   (d) Targets
5. Benefits
   (a) Potential economic benefits
   (b) Other benefits
6. Possible undesirable consequences (where possible suggesting steps to overcome or minimize them)
7. Barriers to programme (e.g., disadvantages as seen by farmers and steps taken to overcome them)
8. Extension strategy: a statement of the kind of information to be conveyed, any special points to be emphasized and the advisory methods to be used
9. Co-operation with other ministries and organizations
10. Evaluation procedure: how progress is going to be evaluated; who is going to do it

---

Work planning

A Work Plan is your plan of operations. It will cover the way you use your resources and will include the following considerations:

Staff	– how many, to do what, when?
Training	– who requires it, when, where, how long?
Media communications	– what is required, where will it be obtained?
Equipment	– what you need and where?
Farm inputs	– what and where?
Marketing	– have market organizers been informed of the plans?
Transport required	– where, when?
Administration	– are there clerks and storemen available, or needed?

Finance — who controls funds, pays? What security arrangements are there?

Technical information

The next step is to package the technical information which will be required by Change Agents and farmers. This will obviously include details about the innovations proposed. This information should be in the form of pamphlets or technical manuals. It takes some time to collect this information and to write it in a suitable form; therefore work on it should start very early in the programme.

Without appropriate information, staff and farmers cannot be trained and the details of the programme cannot be worked out. Lack of appropriate technical information is a major cause of project failures.

Evaluation

You have to decide how the programme will be supervised and how it will be evaluated. To evaluate is to judge numerically an activity or happening. It also has a broader meaning which includes a judgement of the effect the activity has on people, both materially and in their behaviour.

We can evaluate the effect of a programme by the increased wealth or goods people have, the changes in their work and living style, and the change in their attitudes. We should evaluate, because it is important to know whether or not time or money have been wasted on doing something.

The evaluation will guide us in our future planning.

When to evaluate

Evaluation is usually considered an activity to undertake after a programme is completed. However, evaluation is best undertaken in three stages:

(a) Before the programme starts in order to provide base line data and guide the programme (pre-evaluation).

(b) During the programme (on-going evaluation), this allows adjustment to be made to the programme before it is too late.

(c) At the end of the programme (post-evaluation).

This final evaluation allows the entire programme to be assessed, which provides a basis for reporting the programme, and gives guidance for similar future programmes.

Thus, it is important to evaluate the programme even if it is considered a failure. Planners need to know why the programme failed to prevent making future mistakes.

Pre-evaluation (before the programme)

You must consider what the programme is trying to achieve and what are its objectives. These objectives show what to do the base line study on.

If, for example, the objective is 'to increase production of milk by 50 per cent, by increasing the number of cows, by using improved pastures, by using fertilizer and cattle feed', then obviously you should study the local dairy farming situation. You will need to get some information about the dairy farmers, their numbers, attitudes and present practices (such as how pastures are now managed, what fertilizer is used and what feed stuffs, and what are the present yields).

Figure 32   Reasons for programme failure

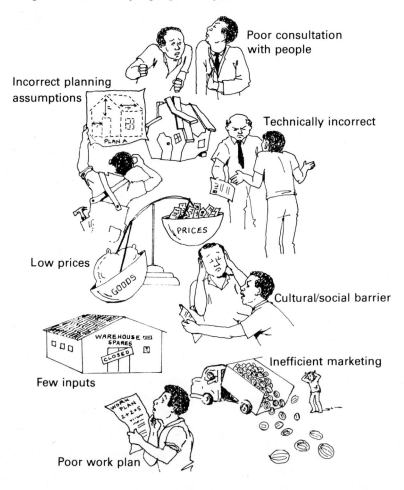

On-going evaluation (during the programme)
When planning, you must decide how regularly the on-going evaluation should be made. By comparing the base line study with the results so far obtained, the evaluator can see where the programme is succeeding or failing. Programmes need to be flexible, not rigid, and if the evaluation shows that certain aspects of the programme are not working, then programme organizers will have to try to amend the plan.

Post-evaluation (at end of the programme)
The same evaluation steps should be undertaken as for the on-going evaluation, but in greater depth. Particular care should be taken in examining possible side effects of the programme. If the side effects have been very damaging, then similar on-going programmes may have to be modified or abandoned.

Self-study questions

1. One of the best practical ways of learning about agricultural planning is to undertake a farm study. Spend a day with a progressive farmer to collect data (technical, economic and social) and a day with a poor farmer. Use the farm report form. Later on, sessions with a supervisor can be held to discuss the problems identified.
2. What is an Extension programme plan?
3. Why is a plan necessary?
4. What types of evaluation are there?
5. How does evaluation help in Extension work?
6. Write two clear and comprehensive objectives about two innovations in your own area.

9 Rural development strategies

As professional rural development people we must understand the theoretical basis of selecting development strategies. This chapter looks at the possible development needs of a rural community and how these needs can be assessed. We consider what development strategies can be adopted to meet these needs and then focus on extension strategies. We are particularly concerned with the assumptions sometimes made by planners of Extension programmes.

Objectives

By the end of the chapter the reader should be:
   (a) Familiar with the possible development needs of a rural community.
   (b) Aware of the different development strategies that can be selected to satisfy these needs.

Definitions of words used

assumption	– a point taken for granted, accepted without question
constraint	– confinement, barrier
development strategy	– a plan for the progress of an area
infrastructure	– supporting framework, including such things as transport, marketing, postal and banking systems in use.

Introduction: Inputs and services to assist development

Before making any decisions about what development strategy should be followed in a particular situation, you should be aware of human and natural resources of the area, and the needs and ambitions of the community (Chapter 8).

You also need to know what are the specific inputs and services that could be provided to assist a community. All communities are likely to need different inputs from each other, depending on their farming systems, infrastructure, knowledge, motivations, etc.

The development strategy chosen, then, should be dependent on

the inputs and services required, as well as those which are available.
Examples of development inputs and services:
(a) Farm inputs, e.g., seed, fertilizer, machinery
(b) Credit
(c) An attractive price for products
(d) Marketing/transport/storage
(e) Infrastructural development (roads, bridges, electricity, etc.)
(f) Land reform/fair tenancy agreements
(g) Water control and fair allocation
(h) Motivation of people (visits, meetings, media)
(i) Technical information for farmers
(j) Media information services
(k) Farmer training
(l) Farmer representation in decision making and planning

Provision of services

The question of what kind of organization should provide the services required has to be answered. In some cases the best role for government may be to encourage other organizations to be active. Whilst an Extension service may be suitable in many circumstances, in another situation a different strategy may be necessary. These strategies include encouragement of the commercial sector, encouragement of farmer co-ops, and improved rural information services. In some countries at a later stage of development, such organizations can often provide a better service than government.

Constraints to development

Development efforts may fail, not because the efforts were insufficient, but because the farmers were unable or unwilling to change due to social or infrastructural constraints. These constraints may have to be removed before development can take place, and Extension may be ineffective until this has been done. These constraints may include unfair tenancy agreements, high credit charges, low produce prices or poor marketing.

Some planners believe that training will solve all development problems, assuming that the ignorance of farmers is the cause. A. Fuglesang, a noted expert in adult education, writes: 'Our educators are taught – and teach – that ignorance is the cause of poverty. This sustains the deception that a structural change in society to eliminate the deeper causes is not necessary' (*About Understanding*).

Once these structural constraints, or some of them, are removed then progress can be quite rapid. The increased demand for services, information and training is then likely to be very considerable. However, while the constraints remain, development plans will fail, and much money and effort will have been wasted. There are many examples of this throughout the world.

Figure 33   Development inputs and services

Communities and individuals also differ in their needs as their circumstances change. Thus the inputs and services chosen must suit the particular circumstances of the community. For example, a well motivated community may only require technical information and credit, while another community may require an Extension service, farm inputs, better roads and markets.

Development strategies

Governments will have to decide what development strategies will best suit the needs of the rural community. This should be based on a careful analysis of the specific requirements. There are a number of possible strategies or combinations of strategies, some of which are described below.

Farm-controlled strategies
    (a) Village selected voluntary agents (usually working part time)
    (b) Village selected agents (paid by farmer co-operatives)

Commercial strategy
    (c) Commercial organizations providing advice and marketing facilities

Government educational-based strategies
    (d) Information transmitted through schools/clubs
    (e) Unit transmitting information via booklets, press, radio, cine, television

Government services
    (f) A visiting service providing motivation and technical advice
    (g) A visiting service providing motivation, technical advice, plus farm inputs, credit, etc.
    (h) An advisory service based on a network of centres usually located near a market and source of farm inputs

Government or commercial highly supervised strategies
    (i) Nucleus estate type development. This is a central farm and processing and packing plant are surrounded by small farmers using the facilities
    (j) Training, credit and input projects for specific crops
    (k) Closely supervised irrigation projects

Large private or commercial estates
    (l) Support to large producers, landowners

Control strategies
    (m) Control and enforcement measures by government

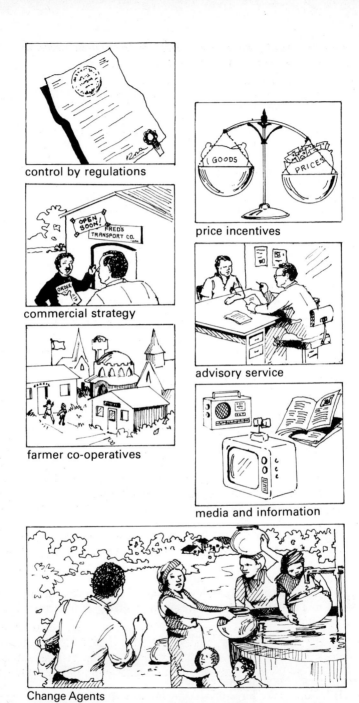

Figure 34 Examples of development strategies

Figure 35 Model showing historical changes in development strategies, as development takes place

Administrative control for taxation purposes	*Simple farming, often slash and burn*
Regulatory control to protect natural resources	*Opening up of new lands*
Government propaganda for increased food production; beginning of Extension services	*Increase in town populations*
Extension supervisory services	*Some progressive farmers, use of sprays, improved seed, fertilizer*
Advisory services and media	*Many farmers seeking advice; better farming taking place*
Commercial services, farmer co-ops and media	*Intensive, specialized production; good farming*

Assumptions about Extension

Some assumptions about Extension made by planners may be incorrect and not based on sound reasons. Sometimes insufficient facts are know about the situation.

For example, in an East African country in 1981 farmers were failing to bring their cattle to the dip in order to kill the disease-carrying ticks. The assumption was made by the Extension planners that the farmers were ignorant of the need to dip cattle. In fact, the dip attendants were stealing half the dip chemical thus rendering the dipping process ineffective: this the farmers realized.

You must carefully identify and examine any assumptions to consider how valid they may be. Also you need to remember that what may be true for one area may not be true somewhere else.

Self-study activities

1. Assumptions about Extension: Below are listed some of the assumptions commonly made about Extension. Check them to see if you consider them valid, particularly for your own area. Some comments have been made about each assumption listed. Do you agree with the comments?

   (a) *That Extension can pass research results to farmers*
   Research results need first to be tested in the field before being recommended to farmers. Who should do this, research or

Extension? At present nobody seems to be responsible. Often Change Agents do not have information about relevant past research. Who should supply this?

(b) *That Extension is the main information source for farmers*
In some countries farmers obtain most of their information from the radio, newspapers and other media, or from other farmers or commercial sources such as shopkeepers, and not from Change Agents. Research indicates that the farmer is most receptive to information just before a sale (insecticide, fertilizer, seed, etc.). Do we make use of this fact? Should Extension personnel work more closely with market and shop people?

(c) *That Extension services are efficient and effective*
Can middle class, formally-educated, town-oriented Change Agents really have much empathy with poor, illiterate, suspicious farmers? In some societies the peasants are regarded with indifference and as a group of people who should not or cannot be helped, but rather should be exploited for the benefit of the middle and upper classes. In some countries some people believe that, once you have obtained a post with government, you are not really expected to work, but are simply entitled to your salary. Should these services improve their selection processes, taking into account the applicants' character and attitudes rather than their educational and social background?

(d) *That Extension should help the very poorest farmers*
Is this a viable idea? Do the poorest farmers want help? Is there leadership amongst the poorest groups or can it be developed? Can strong groups be formed? Should we help the village as a whole rather than a part? Extension planners must carefully examine whether they want to deal with separate sections of the farming community or with the farming community as a whole. The policy may vary from community to community.

(e) *That Extension should encourage farmers to maximize their production*
Development organizations usually consider that high input farming aiming at high yields is in the best interests of the farmer. Their efforts are concerned with encouraging farmers to obtain high yields from one or two crops.

However, Change Agents are beginning to realize that many farmers consider it much more important to minimize the risk of crop failure. A small farmer is often concerned that if he overextends himself by borrowing money for inputs, then in the event of complete or partial crop failure, he may be bankrupt and unable to feed his family. Indeed, he may then lose his land. Thus a farmer will have several planting dates in order to minimize crop loss because of uncertain rains. He will also plant a number of different crops for the same reason. His primary concern is survival. Once his food supply is assured, he may be prepared to grow cash crops, but not before.

If the above is true how should it affect our planning and advice?

2. List the services which may be required by a community for the purposes of agricultural development.
3. Define 'needs assessment'.
4. When and why might certain development strategies be preferable to others? Give examples.